Also by Ellen DeGeneres

My Point . . . And I Do Have One

ellen degeneres

the funny thing is . . .

simon & schuster paperbacks

new york london toronto sydney

SIMON & SCHUSTER PAPERBACKS
Rockefeller Center
1230 Avenue of the Americas
New York, NY 10020

First Simon & Schuster paperback edition 2004

SIMON & SCHUSTER PAPERBACKS and colophon are registered trademarks
of Simon & Schuster, Inc.

For information about special discounts for bulk purchases,
please contact Simon & Schuster Special Sales at
1-800-456-6798 or business@simonandschuster.com

Designed by Jaime Putorti

Manufactured in the United States of America

9   10   8

The Library of Congress has cataloged the hardcover edition as follows:
DeGeneres, Ellen.
The funny thing is— / Ellen Degeneres.
p.   cm.
PN6165 .D44 2003
2003059200
ISBN 0-7432-4761-2
ISBN 0-7432-4763-9 (Pbk)

acknowledgments

This book is not only a labor of love but a legal, contractual agreement. Writing a book is not like writing for an HBO special. It's different. There's punctuation:-!?, spelling, and grammar. It's hard work, and this would not be the book it is without the following people.

First and foremost, Rob Weisbach, my editor (for two books now), and still a friend. Eric Gold, Eddy Yablans, Harley Neuman, and Kevin Yorn, my peeps and my posse. Karen Kilgariff, Karen Anderson, Andrea Levin, my muses. Alex Herschlag, my longtime friend and supporter. Craig Peralta, my savior. Betty and Elliott DeGeneres, my creators, and Alexandra Hedison, my inspiration. And all of my fans for the love and support.

Thank you all.

table of contents

table of contents

the funny thing is . . .

a message from the author

hello, and welcome to my new book. Please make yourself at home while you read it: Take off your shoes, loosen your pants, make those funny at-home faces that we all make. Be comfortable. On the other hand, if you're reading this in a more public place—a plane, a train, a jurors' box during a trial—it might serve you better to be a little less comfortable. Oh, and if you're reading this while you're driving, PUT THE BOOK AWAY! YOU'RE DRIVING, FOR PETE'S SAKE! But wherever you're reading this book, please remember to turn off your cell phone and that the taking of flash photographs is strictly forbidden.

Now, you may want to know why I'm writing this book. Well, there are a number of very good reasons, most of which I forgot the moment I sat down to write. I have a vague recollection of losing a bet to Al Roker, so that may be one of the reasons. Also, I don't have anything to do for a year as I wait to start my new talk show. People have suggested that I simply enjoy the time off—I'll be wishing for this next year. People (different people—not the same ones) have also suggested I read books.

The fact is, I'd rather write a book than read a book. It's like reading, only you get paid for it. Otherwise, it has all the same elements. I don't know what's on the next page. It's suspenseful, yet I can control where it goes. It's like interactive reading. Besides, I've already read books. A lot of them. Well, definitely more than seven.

One thing that you should know if you ever get tired of reading books and decide to write one on your own (I would suggest doing this only and I mean *only* after you finish this book): writing a book is hard work. You can't just sit there staring at the computer screen and wait for words to magically appear. Believe me—I tried doing that for five months and I didn't get a single word.

Suddenly, all this talk about "writing a book" is making me feel overwhelmed. I need to take a break. Excuse me.

Okay, I'm back. I went to brush my teeth (just three of them—I never do them all at once). That, by the way, is an excellent way to pass the time. Hygiene is important anyway, as we all know. So take your time and brush, then floss. Flossing is key. You must floss. Don't even think for a second that you can get away with not flossing. Always floss. I can't stress it enough.

If you get nothing else from this book, I hope you not only think to yourself "I must floss," but pass it along to loved ones and acquaintances—floss, floss, floss. Now, what was I saying?

Oh yes, Why another book?

Seriously, why? There are so many books already. What could I possibly have to say that needs to be read by millions or at least hundreds of people? Perhaps you're reading this to get never-before-revealed insights into who I am as a person. If so, here's a good one for you, right off the bat: If anyone knows me at all, they know I enjoy the smell of a freshly washed monkey.

Or perhaps you're hoping to learn a thing or two. I have no brand-new words to put out there (unless you count "fuzlart," which between you and me is a made-up word), no insights on the meaning of life or even how to be content most of the time.

I have been interested in some deeper meaning of this existence for a long time. I assume we all are, judging by the sales of books devoted to helping us find the answers. I have all of them, but I haven't found one that says anything very different. They all sort of say the same thing.

I suppose I could put down my own ideas of what I think would be at least a good start for happiness, if you're interested. Oh, you are? Okay then.

1. Be nice to everyone, even though you don't want to and you may not like certain people. Be kind, friendly, and respectful even if people are not nice to you. That way, you're not dragged down to their level. Also, there's noth-

ing that annoys arrogant jerks more than people being nice to them.

2. Floss, every day floss. As discussed. In addition to aforementioned perks, flossing encourages healthy gums and makes your teeth feel secure when they're eating something difficult like apples or corn on the cob.

3. Try to have some quiet time every day. I know it's hard, don't tell me. It's getting to be near impossible to find silence, what with the TV, radio, kids, leaf blowers, helicopters, traffic, birds, dogs barking, your grammy yelling from the back of the car, "Stop flossing, you're going to get us all killed!!!" (Seriously, when I told you not to read while you were driving, I didn't mean you should floss instead.) But try to put time aside to listen to "you." It's easy to forget what "you" want, who "you" are, with all the noise. Check in with "you" every day (or at least on New Year's Eve).

4. Exercise. Any form of movement will do. Stretching keeps you limber, young, and energized. My favorite exercise is walking a block and a half to the corner store to buy fudge. Then I call a cab to get back home. (There's never a need to overdo anything.)

5. Drink lots of water. I can't function unless I drink a lot of water. My favorite way to drink water is to put it in a tray, make ice cubes, then put one of those cubes into a big ol' glass of scotch. Let's have some now, shall we?

Thinking back (a good thing to do while drinking scotch), I knew I wanted to write this book because I've always loved writing, especially cursive. It's so pretty, all the loops and whatnot. I thought about having this entire book printed in capital letters, so, as the narrator, IT WOULD SEEM LIKE I'M SHOUTING THE WHOLE TIME. I LIKE THE IDEA OF ME SHOUTING INSIDE OTHER PEOPLE'S HEADS. IT MAKES ME FEEL POWERFUL.

You know, it's hard work to write a book. I can't tell you how many times I really get going on an idea, then my quill breaks. Or I spill ink all over my writing tunic. No wonder I drink so much! Then I get so drunk, I can barely feed the baby.

That's what I call myself when I'm drunk, "The Baby."

Okay, I'm putting the drink down. Back to the happiness list . . .

6. Know you are special. How do you know that? Because you bought this book. You are already two steps ahead of the losers who didn't buy this book. They aren't special. When they finally do buy this book, then they too will be special because they have chosen this book, but you will still be two or three or even more steps ahead. Just know when you buy this book, you're ahead.

   Imagine being the last person to buy this book. I pray that doesn't happen to anyone. If word keeps spreading about the magical powers of this book, the joy it gives, the wonders, the life-affirming, the life-changing results of reading this book, no one will ever be last. It will be sold forever and ever and that will make me happy.

7. The key to life is balance. Think of a seesaw. On one side is Give, the other side Take. If you just give and give and give, you've got nothing left. You're empty. Which means you don't weigh anything because empty equals weightless; so Take is just sitting on the ground bored out of its mind saying, "I'm bored, I can't take anymore of this," which is a pretty strong statement since that's what Take's job is. It is to take. And if Take can't take anymore, then well, I think you see my point.

    And the same goes for taking too much. If you keep taking and taking and taking, you get loaded down. Taking equals heavy. So Give is stranded way up in the air saying, "Hey, I'm way up in the air." And then Take is like, "So?" And Give is like, "I hate you. All you do is take." And Take is like, "You're the stupid poopoohead for giving all the time." And Take gets off the seesaw to leave and Give goes crashing to the ground and then Take feels bad and rushes over to see if Give is okay and then they hug and start crying and both apologize for being so selfish. So you see, it needs to be balanced.

8. Minimize stress. When I'm stressed out, I get so stressed. When I'm relaxed, it's a whole different story. I find that life can be difficult. Also, when certain events occur, it can bring on stress. Small things—a car accident, let's say—

can change your whole mood. Everything can be going just fine. You're at home feeling cozy, watching TV. You suddenly remember you're running low on ice cream, jump in your Cutlass Supreme, and you're singing along to some classic Hall & Oates song, and Bam!! Right into the back of some idiot's car. What are they doing stopped there anyway? It's a stop sign, not a red light. You're not supposed to sit there forever. And all the questions start flying at you. Do you have insurance? Have you been drinking? Why are you in your pajamas? Wow, people are nosy. No wonder I rarely leave the house. It's a jungle out there.

9. Start thinking positively. You will notice a difference. Instead of "I think I'm a loser," try "I definitely am a loser." Stop being wishy-washy about things! How much more of a loser can you be if you don't even know you are one? Either you are a loser or you are not. Which is it, stupid?

10. Don't look in the mirror . . . ever.

11. Work, but have playtime. Recess. We lose our play, our fun, all of our joy. We used to say, "Mom, I'm going out to play." Now it's, "Honey, I'm going off to work." We don't see a forty-five-year-old man saying, "I'm going out to play." If he did, his girlfriend or boyfriend would say, "What the heck does that mean? No you won't." You don't see a grown-up squatting on the ground with

a stick poking at ants. If you do, you cross the street. You walk far away from them. You don't see adults lying in the grass staring at the sky saying, "I see bunny rabbits." That is, unless they're on drugs.

So there you have it, your very own book on the keys to happiness, courtesy of me.

Whew, it's a relief that's over. I tell you, writing a book is a bear! Anyway, I hope that you enjoyed reading this book as much as I enjoyed writing it. But before I say "good night," let me— Oh, excuse me, that's the phone. Let me get it, in case it's important. So, I'm putting you on hold . . . now.

Okay, I'm back. That was my editor. Apparently they want this book to be more than eight pages. I guess I've got a little work to do. Suddenly I'm not so happy anymore. I'd better reread this chapter.

And perchance, floss.

the brunch bunch

I'm exhausted. Today is Monday, so of course that means yesterday was Sunday, which naturally means the weekly Sunday brunch at my house. I can't even remember how or when we started this darn thing, but it is Ka-ray-zee with a capital "K." You never know what's going to happen, who's going to say what, or who will show up with whom.

Everybody brings something, so I don't have to do all of the cooking. It's a big relief, especially since I can't cook. I guess if I did cook one Sunday, that would end the whole tradition once and for all. But even though everyone brings a dish, it's still a lot of people and a lot of cleanup. We have the regulars—Paula Abdul, Diane Sawyer, Gloria Steinem, Donatella Versace, Ed Begley Jr., and Eminem—but occasionally someone will bring a guest.

Yesterday Diane Sawyer showed up with Siegfried or Roy (I'm not sure which one). He was wearing something sparkly and kept calling me "darling." He was sweet. One more guest would have been okay except that Paula brought her dry cleaner, who also called me "darling." I don't think a dry cleaner should call me "darling." He should just call me what everyone else calls me: Miss Ellen. He brought Häagen-Dazs (which was completely melted, and you know you can't refreeze that stuff or it gets gross).

Next, Ed walked in with Tara Lipinski, the skater, who was wearing a skating outfit, which I thought was weird. I made a joke, "Oh, I'm sorry, I don't have a rink."

She said, rather flatly, "I'm not skating." Then, after a long silence that made everyone uncomfortable, the dry cleaner asked if he could use my "little girls' room."

So Eminem said, "What are you, a little girl? Are you a little bitch?"

"Em." (I call him "Em." I even call him "Auntie Em," like from the *Wizard of Oz,* and he laughs—sometimes.) "Em," I said, "don't start." He went back to pouring his gazpacho into a soup tureen.

Ed apologized for being late and not calling to alert us that he was bringing an extra guest. He didn't think it would be a big deal, not realizing that a few other people would do the same thing, which, in turn, turned it into a big deal. I just don't have the seating to accommodate nine people. I have a table for six and if one extra shows up, we squeeze in. But now three people would have to eat at the coffee table in the next room, which was awkward, like eating at the kids' table at Christmas or Thanksgiving. Who would it be?

Gloria said she would sit in the other room but not with Eminem. (They don't get along.) Ed offered to join Gloria, but no one else offered. I was just about to volunteer when Diane said she would eat at the coffee table, but only if I promised to play darts with her when brunch was over. I knew she'd say that. Diane Sawyer is really good at darts. Like *weirdly* good. We played once while we were on summer vacation in Scotland and she beat every man at the Hound and Strumpet pub in Glasgow. It was great in retrospect, but at the time, it felt kind of dangerous. Anyway, I was left to sit and eat with Donatella Versace, Siegfried or Roy, Paula Abdul, Paula Abdul's dry cleaner, Tara Lipinski, and Eminem.

For the first twenty minutes we ate in silence, with the exception of the dry cleaner remarking, "This gazpacho is heavenly." He pronounced "gazpacho" with a soft "g," ("jazpacho"), not a hard "g," the way it should be pronounced. I don't care where you're from (and I'm pretty sure he was from Canada), there's no reason you can't get it right.

Every time he said it (I think nine times in twenty minutes), I thought Eminem was going to explode. It was almost as if the dry cleaner was mocking Em's gazpacho—and it's his special recipe! He brings it every week. After the third or fourth time the dry cleaner said "jazpacho," I said, "It's good gazpacho" saying it correctly with the hard "g," hoping he'd realize his stupid mistake, but he just kept on as if *I* was saying it wrong. Even Donatella Versace says it right and she says everything wrong.

Well, when conversation finally began to flow, it was not pleasant. It started harmlessly enough with Siegfried or Roy asking why Paula hangs out with her dry cleaner. Were they friends beforehand and now he just happens to dry-clean her clothes? Did they start chatting when she went to pick up her "outfits," as he called them? And if so, why wouldn't her assistant pick up her "outfits"? Paula just stared at Siegfried or Roy with this kind of knowing smile, like she was "onto him"—you know, the way Paula does. Well, this unnerved everyone and I think the dry cleaner got a little defensive on Paula's behalf. He started questioning Siegfried or Roy on his own "outfits" and from there it led to why Tara Lipinski was wearing her "outfit." Tara didn't understand what he was talking about. It's all she ever wears.

The whole thing escalated into someone (I suspect it was the silent but deadly Paula) throwing a pork chop, which missed everyone at our table but flew clear into the other room, hitting Gloria Steinem in the eye. She screamed out, "Okay, Eminem, you misogynist," assuming it was him. I honestly can't say who it really was because I was getting another helping of creamed corn when it all happened. Anyway, all hell broke loose and it ended with everyone leaving at once.

In all the confusion Ed Begley Jr. backed his electric car into Donatella Versace's Bentley. (Those electric cars sure can build up speed!) It did some damage, but not as much as Eminem driving over my lawn in his LeMans and plowing down my newly planted rose garden. The dry cleaner was at Siegfried or Roy's car exchanging cleaning tips and I was left with a mess to clean up. Well, my housekeeper was—but still!

Tara Lipinski called this morning to see if she had left her purse. I told her she hadn't come with a purse, and she argued she had indeed come with a purse. I said, "No, you didn't. We all commented on your skating attire like you were getting ready to perform or something, remember?"

She said, "Oh, is that what you meant by you don't have a rink? I'm sorry I answered so rudely. I didn't get the joke. Everyone always wants me to skate for them, so I just assumed you were expecting me to skate."

I said, "No, it was a joke."

She said, "Oh . . ." and laughed hysterically until she started choking and whispered she had to go and hung up.

A few minutes later I found a purse in my kitchen and felt so bad that I had been so adamant about her not having brought one. I opened it, hoping to find a phone number for her but when I found the driver's license it was Gloria Steinem's—only her real name is Debbie! Oh, the secrets we keep. . . .

Next Sunday should be interesting.

that's why prison wouldn't be so bad

Sometimes, when I'm trying to get dressed, I find myself just staring at my clothes for an hour. I have not a clue as to what I should put on. It is so hard to decide what to wear. And it got me thinking: *That's why prison wouldn't be so bad.*

Sometimes I don't want to be a grown-up. I don't want to have too many obligations. I don't want responsibilities or deadlines. In prison, I wouldn't have to make any decisions. Life would be so simple.

It's true that the beds don't look very comfortable and they only have those wool blankets. They're itchy. Oh, and the lack of privacy with the bathroom situation? I'd hate that. Then again, they do have TV and a gym. I'd be in excellent shape, probably better than the time I trained for a marathon. They have a fantastic physical-conditioning area and it's outdoors!

How refreshing. They call it the "exercise yard," a yard dedicated to getting fit. You always hear that people in prison are really muscular, but I don't think I'd use the exercise yard for that. I'd probably just want to work on my abs and my cardiovascular. You probably have to bring your own towel and workout gloves, but that's the price you pay for absolutely no responsibility.

There is also the fact that the food is free and I always think free food tastes the best. Like when you go to those hotel manager's receptions. Even though the food is *taquitos* and Swedish meatballs, they're free and actually pretty good. The thing with prison food that might worry me is that someone might try to poison a prisoner and I might accidentally get the plate that was meant for the intended victim. That would be bad. But let's just say I lived through that. Well then, I could probably live through just about anything! Think what a strong constitution I would have. And probably a new zest for life. What's so bad about prison? That's what I wanna know.

I suppose I'd probably have to be someone's bitch. Unless, of course, I got in with the right crowd in the beginning. Still, I'm sure I'd have to do stuff I wouldn't want to do, like rub people's prison feet. Or clean the bathroom with a toothbrush. Maybe I'm thinking of *Private Benjamin* or *Stripes*. I get prison movies confused with army movies—they both have "Lights out!" By the way, lights out would be fine with me. I have an itty bitty book light that I could use to read old magazines, because I think you only get old magazines in jail. I wouldn't have to keep up to date anyway; doing time means not knowing what time or day it is. I doubt I'd even wear a watch. The guards tell you when to do everything. To me that's just another prison perk— I'd never be late for an appointment. And I'd never be early either. (I hate getting somewhere too early, because I never know what to do with myself.) Prison makes so much sense. It seems like I'm the only one who has figured it out.

Granted, it's probably not all that it's cracked up to be. For one thing, I most likely would get into at least one fight, even if I kept to myself and minded my own business. I've heard of those pillowcase fights they have in prison, but they're not the kind you have at a slumber party. In prison they fill the cases up with soda cans and beat you severely. That's an ingenious weapon when you think about it—it's really making the most of your resources. I hope I don't get beaten.

They say your best offense is a great defense, so I'd definitely have to be tough in prison. I would probably start smoking. That's not good, but it would give me something to trade.

I bet I'd get a lot more reading done. I would become a lot smarter by catching up on the classics. You know I've never read *The Sound and the Fury?* Prison would be the perfect opportunity! And I could finally get my GED—finally graduate from high school. Wait a minute. I already graduated. I guess I could get my bachelor's degree and then my master's, maybe a Ph.D. in something. I could really make a lot of money when I get out.

Also think about how many great friends I would make. Lifelong friends. I'd be sure not to make any friends who were in for petty theft. It would be too hard on me to lose them when they get paroled. If I did make friends who were in for small-time crimes, hopefully they would be repeat offenders. Then every time they'd get released I could look forward to seeing them in the near future.

I wonder if I would have a pen pal? A lot of criminals get pen pals. I guess some people love to write letters, but I don't know anyone who does. I love to get mail (not bills—just regular mail), but nobody writes anymore. Prison would be just the ticket to strike up some sort of correspondence. I'd compile everything and make a book out of all the letters. I could call it "Letters from the Pen."

What could I do to be sent to prison? I wouldn't want to hurt anybody, but that would be a surefire way. Who could I kill? Maybe I would just attempt to kill them. How much time would I get for attempted murder? What if it's not enough time to get my Ph.D.?

I could rob a bank, too. Armed robbery with attempted murder . . . that's good. And if I'm lucky enough to get away with it, I'd have the money from the bank robbery, so I wouldn't need my Ph.D. You know what? Now that I think about it, even if I got my Ph.D. I would have to work, and working would mean obligations and responsibilities, so I may as well just go to prison for life.

I'd still read all those books. I would be real smart, and I'd be less stressed because I wouldn't have all that pressure about what to wear. Without the stress, I'd probably look better too. Although who cares how you look? You're in prison—you're in the slammer—the joint—the big house—the clink—the cement Hilton—the lockup—the cooler—the jewelry box—the crate and barrel—the corked jug—the honey pot.

In prison, you have nothing to do all day. I suppose you do have to make your bed. But it's a cot. How long could that take—two minutes? Then you've got another twenty-three hours and fifty-eight minutes of no obligations, no responsibilities, and no deadlines—that is, except license plate making, and frankly that's the easiest job I've ever heard of. Easier than comedy.

Oh man, prison would be sweet. But for now I'm on the outside, and I'll just have to deal with it the best I can.

It's all I know.

my most embarrassing case scenario

The other day a man asked me, "What's the most embarrassing thing that's ever happened to you?" I thought for a minute about the right way to respond and finally settled on, "Would you please leave the ladies' room?" He informed me that not only was I not in the ladies' room, I was actually in his house.

Eventually the whole mess was settled when I explained that I had a severe case of myopia, or "near-sightedness," as the kids like to say, but I was too vain to wear my glasses. Also, my hair had been kind of flat that day and the combination of flat hair and glasses made me look a little like a John Denver impersonator. He understood completely—first, because he was a highly evolved man and second, because I'd already started writing him a blank check for whatever amount he thought would be fair to keep the whole humiliating debacle out of the papers.

Anyway, it got me thinking. There are all sorts of books offering advice on how to deal with life-threatening situations, but where's the advice on dealing with embarrassing ones? I mean, things like landing a burning plane, wrestling a crocodile, or jumping from a moving train happen maybe five, six times in your life. But if you're like me, embarrassing things happen hundreds of times each day. I'm too busy being embarrassed to write a whole book on the subject, but here are a few things I've learned about how to survive life's embarrassing moments.

Note: As there are more embarrassing situations than can be noted in one chapter (an independent research company that I made up and then hired puts the figure of possible embarrassing situations somewhere between a gazillion and one and a half-bazillion), I have chosen five at random. And by random I mean, of course, the ones that have happened to me within the last hour.

SITUATION:
FORGETTING SOMEONE'S NAME

You're at a party. Don't ask me how you were invited. Either your host is very forgiving or he has a very short memory. Or else he realizes that it was partially his fault. Why else would he be bragging about his new fireproof mattress if he didn't expect you to try it out? And yes, in hindsight it is pretty obvious that just because the mattress is fireproof doesn't mean that the sheets and irreplaceable antique quilt are fireproof as well. Anyway that's all water under the bridge (the same water, in fact, that you threw the burning quilt into to put it out).

Anyhoo, you're at the party, you notice an old friend walking toward you, and you start to panic: You've forgotten your friend's name! (I added the exclamation point to make it doubly exciting. Try it yourself. It's fun!) Now, when I say "an old friend" I mean a friend you've known for a long time, not someone who is really old. Someone really old is not much of a problem because one, by the time they mosey on over to you with their walker you'll have had time to go home, look up their name in your address book, then scurry on back to the party without them noticing. And two, there's a good chance they've forgotten their own name as well. I'm talking about someone with a good memory moving toward you at a brisk pace. What do you do? What do *you* do?

Solution

There are a few possible solutions to the "forgetting the name" problem. And I'm not talking about ridiculous ones like pretending to faint, then claiming you don't speak English. That's not only silly, but it has been proven not to work after the incident when you set fire to your host's bedroom.

One solution is to have the same nickname for everyone.

That way you only have to remember one name. The obvious problem with this is that in the throes of passion you don't want to be yelling out "Scooter!" or "Itchy!"

A second solution is to say hi to your old friend, then immediately grab hold of a third person and say all innocentlike, "You two know each other, right?" You wait for them to introduce themselves, and then sit back and relax. The problem with this option is if the third person just answers, "No, I don't know this person." Now you find yourself in the doubly awkward position of having to introduce two people whose names you've forgotten. (And don't get all smart with me and try to say that you know the other person's name—you don't.) I mean, you can always just say, "Scooter, this is Itchy. Itchy, Scooter." But chances are that isn't going to work.

The best solution: Say to her, "I'm sorry, remind me again how you pronounce your name?" To which she'll respond, "Kathy." Then you continue your clever ruse by saying, "That's right, the emphasis is on the first syllable, *Ka*-thy. I always think it's on the second, Ka-*thy*. I'm glad you corrected me, my old friend." Problem solved!

SITUATION: LOSING YOURSELF IN THE MIDDLE OF A CONVERSATION

There's a well-known saying that goes, "Wherever you go, there you are." It's a good saying except for one thing: It's just not true!! (I'd like to apologize for the two exclamation points. Yes, they're fun, but sometimes you can overuse fun things and all of a sudden they're not fun anymore. I guess what I'm trying to say is, if I could go back in time, or if I knew how to use the backspace key on my computer, I would eliminate one of the exclamation points. Sorry.) The reason the saying is false is that when our minds are deprived of stimulation they tend to wander. So, yes, you may have gone someplace, but you're not really there at all. You're somewhere else entirely, probably trying to remember the words to the Armour Hot Dogs song.

Now, the type of stimulation the brain needs is not something like being tickled with a feather. The mind is too mature to be amused by that (not so the insides of your knees, which are always up for being tickled). The mind craves interesting conversation. Which brings us back to the party and *Ka*-thy.

Kathy, it turns out, is a bore, which I'm guessing is why you forgot her name in the first place. She's been talking at you for a long time about this and that and you've just drifted off: ". . . fat kids, skinny kids, even kids with chicken pox love hot dogs . . ." You're kind of aware of her mouth moving, but you have no idea what she's saying. Then you hear the words "inhaling mold spores" and, like that—you're back. You have no idea what the subject of the conversation is, and Kathy has just stopped talking. She's staring at you (or slightly to the right of you because of her lazy eye), expecting you to say something. What do you do? *What* do you do?

Solution

Some people might tell you that you could fake Kathy out by nodding your head and saying, "Ummm. Uh, hmmm. Mmmmm. I see. Hmmm mmmm." I am here to tell you that that's not going to work unless she's part of the one-tenth of one percent of the country who can be hypnotized by people humming.

The only proven way to get yourself out of this embarrassing situation is to say something about Gloria Estefan. I'm telling you, as long as you commit to it, she can fit into any conversation. You don't believe me? Here's proof. Kathy is still staring at you waiting for a response while you dutifully consider, then reject the honesty and "hmm, hmm" options. Finally you say, "That sounds a lot like Gloria Estefan." Kathy looks at you funny and says, "What's that got to do with copper plumbing?" To which you respond, "Well, Gloria Estefan is the copper plumbing of the music industry. She's beautiful, reliable, and indestructible. Look how she came back after that bus accident! Are you going to debate me on this?!" And, presto, you're back in the conversation and nobody's the wiser.

SITUATION:
ACCIDENTALLY REVEALING
INTIMATE THOUGHTS TO A STRANGER

Revealing intimate thoughts to a stranger isn't always embarrassing. In fact, sometimes it's downright therapeutic. Many people pay strangers to listen to their darkest fantasies and most perverse secret thoughts. Those strangers are known, of course, as Starbucks baristas. But, like most situations in life, when there is no money changing hands, the chances of being embarrassed multiply significantly.

So you're still at the party, standing next to Kathy and experiencing one of those long uncomfortable silences that only true friends who have nothing to say to one another get to enjoy. Perhaps you make eye contact with the host of the party. A flash of recognition passes over his face, much like the flash that sprang up from his bed when you set it on fire. His face turns ashen (not ashen like the beloved first-edition books that you tried to put out the fire with, but gray and pale) and he runs off. Probably a funny reaction to the onion dip, you think to yourself.

Still looking after the host, you feel the need to reveal something deep and significant to your old friend Kathy. So you say, "My underwear keeps going up my crack." You hear somebody say, "Excuse me?" Then you turn and see not Kathy but a total stranger. (You don't recognize any of her, not even her elbow or a little bit of her ear.) Kathy has ditched you. "That's it," you say to yourself, "I'm going to forget her name again." The stranger looks at you and says loudly, "Did you just say your underwear keeps going into your crack?" People start to look at you. What do you do? What *do* you do?

Solution

Deny, deny, deny! Or, to paraphrase Sergeant Schultz, one of the most beloved Nazi soldiers in television sitcom history, "I know nothing. I said nothing." So, when the stranger asks again if you said your underwear was going up your crack, you calmly look at her and shriek, "No, of course not. Are you kidding? What?! No!"

Now, there is a chance she'll ask, "Then what did you say?" Don't panic. Just think of something that sounds like what you said, and say that instead. For instance, "You misheard me, stranger, what I said was . . . um . . . er . . . my bear keeps going up my crack." If she says incredulously, "Your bear keeps going up your crack?!" well then all bets are off. It's now time for a different strategy: attack, attack, attack. Look at her and say, "Listen, I've had just about enough with the questions. Who are you, anyway? I don't know you. I don't owe you any explanation. You are way too curious for me, old lady. Why don't you go stand next to someone else and eavesdrop on them, you weirdo?!" And that's usually when Kathy comes back and says, "Oh, great, I see you've met our host's grandmother."

SITUATION:
HUG, KISS, OR SHAKE HANDS

Believe it or not, it is as potentially awkward to greet someone whose name you remember as it is to greet Kathy. That's because you never know what physical action to take upon greeting each other. Do you shake their hand? Do you hug them? Do you kiss them? Or, trickiest yet, do you do the complicated hug-kiss combo? What makes this combo tricky is knowing the order of the beats involved. If you think you're going to kiss on the cheek first, then hug, and your friend feels the opposite, you could end up kissing your friend on the ear or, if your friend is very tall, on the chest. Either way is potentially embarrassing. As is sticking out your hand while your friend tries to kiss you, inevitably ending up with a gooey, kiss-drenched hand.

So, you're at the party and the host is approaching you quickly. It's hard to believe you've been at the party long enough to chitchat, have a few drinks, and eat the first piece of his grandmother's birthday cake (looking back, you probably should have waited for them to light it, but you just assumed that they, like you, were forbidden by court order from playing with matches) without saying hi to the host. Now, there he is marching toward you and you have no idea how to greet him. What do you do? What do you *do?*

Solution

The answer to this dilemma is as simple as it is uncomplicated. Let your friend make the first move and respond accordingly (or *accordionly* if you know how to play one). What's important for this strategy to work is to adopt the right stance so that you're ready for whatever physical greeting is about to be laid on you. I recommend legs shoulder-width apart, shoulders leg-width apart, and arms outstretched but with a little bend in the elbow so that you don't look like you're being crucified. If your friend, undertaking the same strategy, approaches you with the same stance, that's okay too. I've had long conversations with people where both of us stood a foot away from each other, our arms outstretched, talking for hours.

SITUATION:
ACCIDENTALLY FLIPPING OFF
JOHN TRAVOLTA

Granted, the odds of this situation happening are fairly low, maybe one in eight at best, but in my book it's best to be prepared. And since it's my book that you're reading, I'm guessing you feel the same.

So, you're at the party standing in the neutral position ready to greet your host, when he surprises you by grabbing your arm, pressing it into your back, and pushing you toward the door, all the while screaming in a high-pitched voice, "What are you doing here, you crazy bed-burning lady person? (For some reason, whenever your host gets mad he talks like Jerry Lewis.)

The next thing you know, you're being thrown out the door and given what your father calls "the bum's rush." You feel hurt, insulted, and angry, especially since your father was at the party and did nothing to stop your humiliation except to say, "Look, she's being given the bum's rush."

So you get in your car and decide to drive until your anger and your buzz from the three dirty martinis you had wears off. You're driving at the legally acceptable twenty miles above the speed limit, when some jerk cuts in front of you going a mere fifteen miles above the limit. Infuriated, you drive past, and give him the finger, flip him the bird, stick him the digit. (I made that last one up; it just seemed that for rhythm there should be three.) Then you open your eyes (I have no idea why you were driving with your eyes closed) and notice that the driver of the car is none other than John Travolta (which I guess is not much of a surprise given the title of this situation). What do you do? *What do you do?*

Solution

This is an easy one. All you have to do is move your arm to your side, raise it up at a forty-five-degree angle, and pump. During the second pump, casually switch your protruding finger from the middle one to the index finger. Suddenly you're no longer flipping John Travolta off, you're doing a touching homage to one of his most beloved movies, *Saturday Night Fever.*

This, according to the unwritten laws of showbiz, officially makes you John Travolta's friend. So you're perfectly within your rights to follow him wherever he's going, get out of your car when he does, and engage him in conversation. Tell him your dreams, your fears, and all the embarrassing things that happened to you at the party. And don't be surprised if after you've told him all this, he looks at you blankly for a beat, then says, "That sounds a lot like Gloria Estefan."

god, what a day!

I have learned in this business not to believe anything that I read or hear about anyone until I sit down with that person and hear it for myself. Fortunately, that's one of the perks of this business—you get to meet a lot of interesting people and you get to have a lot of interesting conversations. I've been lucky enough to meet the President and Oprah and Madonna and a lot of other fascinating people, so it was only a matter of time before I would meet God. And I have. What a day that was!

Imagine my surprise when one afternoon I received an invitation with the return address *God in Heaven*. Here's what it said inside:

> Ellen, please join me for fondue and Chablis.
> When: Saturday May 3rd, 2:00 P.M.

Where: My house
(No need to RSVP. I'll know if you're coming.)

Now, normally I don't like Chablis, but this one was nice. It was dry with a peppery oak aftertaste. But I'm getting ahead of myself.

I was nervous with anticipation for weeks. Finally, the big day arrived and I made my way over to God's house. As I was pulling up, Jennifer Love Hewitt was just leaving. (She is *so* sweet.) I was led into God's living room and told to wait. (It was so bright in there! Let me tell you, every lamp was on—it was crazy, crazy bright!) As I was sitting there, I started to think, *I wonder what he dresses like? Does he wear that robe all the time?* Like the Pope. I mean, he can't *always* wear that Pope outfit, can he? Once in a while, don't you think he throws on a pair of shorts and a tank and just, you know, chills out? And then I started thinking, *I wonder if I'm dressed appropriately to meet God?* I don't know how you are supposed to dress. Then I realized the obvious. God has seen me naked! So I just took my clothes off.

Anyway, I was looking around the living room and in front of me there was a coffee table with two magazines on it, *Teen People* and *Guns & Ammo*, and a poster of a kitten on the wall that says "Hang in There, Baby." And there were pictures of Jesus everywhere! You can't believe how many pictures of Jesus there were. A picture of Jesus on a pony with a cowboy hat. A picture of Jesus on the beach wearing a shirt that says, "My parents created the universe and all I got was this lousy T-shirt."

I started to get nervous. *I'm going to meet God in just a minute,* I thought. *I don't even know how to greet God. Do I shake hands or do I curtsy or bow? I mean, do we hug?* I feel close enough to God to hug God, but I know how it is—a lot of people want to hug me (TV does that), but I don't want to hug a lot of people. You've got to be respectful.

So, a couple of minutes later God walked in the room carrying a tray with a fondue pot and a bottle of Chablis. I would say she was about forty-seven, forty-eight years old, a beautiful, beautiful black woman, and we just immediately hugged. She smelled so good. She said it was Calvin Klein's Obsession.

We sat down and started drinking the Chablis and talking about the weather and what was going to happen to it. I asked her a bunch of questions I was curious about. "What is the hardest thing about being God?"

"Trusting people," she said. "You never know if people really like ya or if it's just because you're God. And people always want something from you. They want money and then they want more money. That's what they always ask for."

She told me nobody ever thanks her anymore. The only people who thank her are boxers and rappers, but she said she thinks it's a little odd that rappers are doing songs like "Slap the Bitch up the Ass," and the next thing out of their mouth is, "I'd like to thank the Lord Almighty for this award. Praise Jesus!"

"Nobody cares about the miracles anymore," she continued. "The miracles just go by unnoticed."

"What was the last miracle?" She started to cry, upset that I had to ask.

"It was the toilet that flushes automatically," she said, her eyes welling up with tears. "Before that it was the George Foreman grill . . . the fat just drips right off."

Well, I guess it was the Chablis making me feel more relaxed or something, but I was loosened up enough to say, "God, I have to admit, I've really felt alone a lot. I've felt like you didn't exist. I just didn't believe in you for a while."

She said, "Do you remember that day you were walking on the beach?"

I said, "Yeah."

"Well, I was there."

"But there was just one set of footprints."

She said, "I was on your back."

"I *thought* I felt heavy that day. I thought it was water retention."

"No," she said. "Know when you are bloated, I am there."

That comforts me.

I'm not going to bore you with everything. We talked about so many things. She told me the meaning of life . . . stuff like that. Suddenly, in the middle of our conversation, she got up and gently put her arms around me and said it was time for me to go. She had another visitor arriving at 3:30, God explained, and had to wash out the wineglasses and prepare more fondue.

As I waved good-bye to her I had such a feeling of inner

peace and tranquillity. I got into my car and noticed that Henry Winkler was walking up to God's door. He gave me a funny look, but it might've been because I was still stark naked.

But who cares? I felt free, finally having a clear picture of just how precious life is, and why we shouldn't let ourselves be strangled by doubt and fear. I also learned something just as valuable. If I could meet God, I thought, I could meet just about anyone or do just about anything. There's no reason to live a life of regret. If I really put my mind to it, if I truly believe, one day I could learn how to macramé.

I can only pray.

gift exchange

or

The Art of Believable Acting

AUTHOR'S NOTE:

Although I've specified the holidays in this chapter, you can apply this advice to all gift-giving and getting situations—except Arbor Day! When it comes to Arbor Day, the only rules are There Are No Rules! *Wait, that might be the rules for spring break. I'll have to check my files.*

Sure, when you first read the title of this chapter you thought, "Come on, Ellen, this is one area of my life where your infinite wisdom and eerie insight are not necessary." But think about it: What time of year is the most stressful, painful, and all-around disappointing? Yes, New Year's Eve! And that's because you're finally releasing all the stress and resentment that the holiday gift-giving season has heaped upon your weary shoulders.

The whole idea of exchanging gifts is much more complicated than most people realize, so stop denying that you need
help, unclench your jaw (see, I know what it feels like), and finish this chapter. You'll never waste another fifty dollars on a last-
minute wine and cheese basket again.

Now, you may be thinking, *Hey, Ellen, even though you're
being very funny and I enjoy your witty insights and lighthearted
ribbing, it really is the thought that counts.* If you are thinking
that, then I thank you for the compliment, but quit your infer-
nal thinking and listen to me for a second.

The saying "It's the thought that counts" was coined as an
emotional Band-Aid by someone who left all of her shopping
until nine o'clock Christmas Eve . . . or the night before the
first day of Hanukah or until right before Kwanzaa or until the
twilight of the day of winter solstice. [*Please write to my publisher if I forgot to include your chosen cultural gift-giving holiday.*]
If it's really the thought that counts, then why don't we ever tell
people what we were thinking when we were scrambling to buy
them their last-minute panic gift? "It was less than twenty dollars and I hardly ever see him that much anyway." We don't say
these things because it's not the thought of the giver that counts.
The "thought that counts" is the thought the getter is thinking
after the wrapping paper has been torn away.

If we were really thoughtful, we would buy presents for people that they could, in turn, give away to the people still left on
their shopping lists. Your friend could unwrap your gift to find
a wrapped gift with his niece's name right on the tag, ready to

go. You just bought him three hours *not* spent in a mall. Now that's thoughtful!

It takes this kind of effort and creativity to figure out what would make a good gift for someone. You have to consider what the person likes, what they already have, what they care about, what they need; basically you have to invest a lot of your time. And since time is the one thing none of us has anymore, we end up giving a box-set of Bailey's Irish Cream liqueur with shot glasses with "Luck o' the Irish" stamped on the front of them. It looks like a gift, it seems like a gift, but no one ever uses, drinks, or looks at it after December 26 . . . or December 8 or the week of the 12th. [*Please write to my publisher if the date you throw away useless gifts was not mentioned above.*]

It wasn't like that back in the good old days, when dear old dad would spend all summer and most of the fall whittling you your own train set out of freshly cut pine. That's back when thoughts really did count and you could go to the movies all day for a nickel and not get kidnapped. But as times will do, times have changed. If you gave a kid a homemade pine train set today, he would sue you for breach of contract. (Why people sign Christmas contracts with their children these days, I will never know.)

Since we can't, as adults, get away with throwing bad presents against a wall and bursting into tears, Christmas is the time of year when we all become really good at lying. Lying is just another form of acting, so in a way, we are all actors in a forty-eight-hour play that runs from the 24th through the 25th of

December. Again, unless you're Jewish, in which case you have to fake it for eight days straight. There are people in Los Angeles who pay thousands of dollars for that kind of rigorous training. Last year, my mother should have at least received a Best Actress nomination for her performance after opening the shoe tree my aunt gave her. It was gritty, real, and heart-wrenching; in short, a tour de force.

Because of this widely accepted deceit, it's very hard to tell if someone really likes the gift you got for them (the eggnog doesn't help either), so here's a quick checklist that you can use. You know, for checking.

How to tell if someone doesn't like the gift you have given them

1. They say, "I love it."

If they say they love it, you can be sure they hate it. Loving a towel rack makes no sense, so clearly they're overcompensating for the feelings of guilt and shame about the deeper feelings of anger and resentment they have about being given a towel rack for Christmas. Or maybe they've gone insane with rage over getting such an impersonal, utilitarian gift after thirty-five years of marriage. (Just a tip: Never give any kind of rack as a gift. I don't care how nice the rack is. Yes, even rack of lamb.)

2. They say, "Thank you."

"Thank you" is such a loaded statement. The nuances are imperceptible, woven with sarcasm, irony, and plain old sass.

The person might as well just spit on your shoe. Special circumstance: If they sigh, shake their head, and stare deeply into your eyes right before they say it, they are an impostor and you should call the police.

3. They say, "Where did you get it?"

The nerve! Why don't they just say, "Does the store give cash refunds so that I can return this and finally get something I actually want?" Quick fix: Buy all your gifts in Japan. That way, nobody wins.

Epilogue: The Myth of Handmade Gifts

Unreturnable, unusable, unsightly, unfun. These are just some of the words you can use to describe handmade gifts. Unless you're related to a talented furniture maker, a clothing designer, or you are someone's grandma, getting a handmade gift for Christmas is *never* not disappointing. Even grandmas secretly hate them, but society forces them to repress their real feelings about being gypped. Instead, they have to pretend they love multicolored, glitter-covered macaroni sculptures. Why do we put the aged through this kind of strain? They just want a DVD player like everyone else.

When considering giving a homemade gift, just think to yourself, *Is this a gift I would like to get?* And then think to yourself, *Why do I still have this leather-burning tool when putting your name on the back of your belt went out of style in 1976?* And then think, *Is it right for me to heap the by-products of my knitting hobby onto my friends and family in lieu of buying them actual gifts that cost actual money?* And then think, *Why am I so selfish? Not just about the crafts, but about everything I do and say. It's always "Me, me, me" and "Look what I can make and look how fast I can knit."*

I never think about what it would be like to receive a scarf with leather piping that has my name burnt into it. It would be creepy and irritating. Especially because when it's wrapped, it's exactly the shape as two bars of gold. There. I think I've said my piece.

With all this in mind, get out there and let the people you care about most (or whose names you drew in the Secret Santa gift exchange at work) know exactly how much you're thinking of them this holiday season by picking out fun, useful, and exciting gifts.

Then, after you've been shopping for two hours and you realize you don't know what your father's interests are, give up and go to the bulletproof option: the gift certificate.

silence is golden

I think people talk too much.

Talk, talk, talk, talk, talk, talk, talk. Sometimes, when people are talking, in my mind all I'm saying is *shut up, shut up, shut up, shut up, blah, blah, blah, blah, blah.* . . .

People are scared of silence. If you find silence, people always have to fill it with something. The world is so full of noise, it's nearly impossible to find silence. I happen to believe that silence is golden. In life, it's one small thing I can hold onto. Silence is where all of our answers are. It's where our truth is. Our passion, our path, our everything . . . All the answers are in silence, if you can find it.

I was outside not too long ago and I tried to meditate. I closed my eyes and I got to that still place that everybody talks about—just for a moment, but I was there. And the first mes-

45

sage that I got, so strongly and so clearly, was that we are all one. Every living thing, we are all connected. And the next thing I felt was this little tiny thing in the palm of my hand, and I opened one eye. I saw this little mosquito sitting there, this little prehistoric-looking creature—this strange bug. And I was thinking about how we are all connected and I looked at this thing and then I just . . . killed it. Then I went back to my loving state of being.

And the next thing I heard was, "Would you like anything else or will that be all?" I told the waiter, "I was meditating, idiot. Thanks a lot for interrupting!" He wasn't getting a tip anyway. It had taken forever to get the veal. So I decided an outdoor café was not the best place to be spiritual. People are too rude and stupid. So I left and started walking to my car, which was about three blocks away. The parking situation is crazy because the world is overpopulated with the wrong kinds of people.

So, back to the loving place. I was walking and I saw my car and I saw a meter maid standing at my car writing a ticket. "Oh please, wait . . . stop. Please don't write the ticket, I'm here," I said.

And she said, "Oh, I'm sorry, but you're parked illegally in front of a fire hydrant."

"Oh! *Illegally in front of a fire hydrant,*" I said, mocking her.

"Please stop talking to me that way," she said.

So I took a different approach. "Please be compassionate, don't give me the ticket, I'm here."

And she said, "Oh, I'm sorry, I've already started writing, I can't stop."

"Oh, that's how it works? You've already started writing, so you can't stop? Okay, well I would like to not hit you but my fist is already in the air, okay?"

And . . . back to the loving place.

I got into my car and lit a cigarette and prayed to be led where I should be, and I heard, "Drive!" (It was the meter maid.)

So I started driving and it's so hard to drive and be compassionate and loving because of the way people drive. I was behind someone and they were going so slow I could have gotten out of my car and walked around and said, "Sorry I have to pass you but you're going a little too slow." Anyway, so I pulled around to give them that "I hate you" look. (How else are they going to learn, right? It's up to us.) And it turns out it was a nun. Can you believe that? I said, "Why don't you take a vow not to drive! Drop it like a bad habit!"

And . . . back to the loving place.

Again I found myself praying to be led where I should be. And then I saw a health food store, just right there. It appeared right before my eyes, and I thought, *Well, that seems spiritual. I've never been in a health food store before.* I don't know if you've ever been in a health food store but if that's healthy, sorry— don't want to be it.

The people who work at these places are so proud of themselves. "Guess how old I am?" they say.

"I don't know."

"Guess, guess."

"Thirty?"

"I'm sixteen, but the point is, I've never had dairy!"

So I go into this health food store and the person at the counter says, "Let me see your tongue."

"What?"

"Let me see your tongue. . . . Oh, you're full of toxins!"

"*You're* full of toxins. What a stupid thing to say to me."

It turns out I needed an herb for something inside me—like the spleen or something else that's inside—because something needed something because of something that happened. I learned this because the health food person practices this thing called kinesiology. They put herbs in your hand and if your arm goes down you need those herbs. This sounds stupid, but actually it's not—it works. I'll tell you, last week I was at Gucci and I had a sweater in my hand and it went right down. A couple of minutes earlier I had a dress in my hand and it didn't go down at all! See? It works.

So, he/she gave me his/her recommendation. (I don't know what he/she was. The name was Earthspirit. What's that? A boy's name?) Earthspirit said, "You need some wheatgrass juice."

"Wheatgrass juice! Do I need a sprout wrap too?"

And Earthspirit said, "Your aura's brown." And I said, "*Your* aura's brown! What a stupid thing to say to me!"

"Oh, we're going to have to call the security guard."

"The health food security guard? What's his name, Whispering Pine? Why, is my meat breath offending you?"

Anyway, they kicked me out.

So I was driving again . . . back to the loving place . . . praying I'd be led to where I was supposed to be, and suddenly a wave of energy hit me. *You're out of rum. If you're quiet, it will come.*

So I went to the liquor store and there was no parking. I had to park across the street in some stupid parking lot (because again, you know, the wrong kind of people . . .). And so I went into the liquor store to get my rum and a pack of smokes and some rolling papers. (Right on! Peace!) I came out, and a parking attendant was standing right next to my car. He hadn't been there when I'd gone into the liquor store but he said, "Oh, you can't park here for that establishment. To park here you have to go into this establishment and purchase something and get validated."

I said, "Oh, please, be compassionate, idiot."

"No, you have to go in here."

So anyway, it looked like a spiritual-type place that I was being led to. It was called the Pleasure Chest or something like that. Some type of toy store, it seemed. Unsafe toys, though, 'cause I've been playing with some of them and I'll tell you, this pogo stick is going to hurt somebody. It's bad on your back and it's not sturdy! So, in order to get my car out from the parking lot, I had to buy something. It was getting late and I didn't want to deal with the traffic and I wanted to get into the carpool lane, so I bought a blow-up doll.

I don't know if I didn't blow it up properly or what, but after a little while it started to deflate. So I had to pull over to the side of the road to inflate it again. (Why they put the valve in the crotch area I don't know. It's silly is what it is. Just silly.)

So there I was on the side of the road, blowin' up "Linda"— I named her—and that's when there was a knock on the window. It was a cop, of course. I thought, *This does not look good at all, you know?* It did not help matters any that I was naked.

Okay, so I'll tell you why I was naked. If you're going to buy a blow-up doll, be forewarned. These dolls do not come with clothes. I don't know what that's about, but there are no clothes—at all! You can't even dress them up. So I thought, *I'm not going to look like a crazy person driving around with a naked passenger. I'm not stupid!* So there I was, naked except for the harness. (I had also bought a harness and a captain's hat and a paddle.) I was standing on the side of the road, getting handcuffed in my harness and captain's hat and paddle, holding Linda, and the cop said, "You have the right to remain silent."

And I said, "Finally, that's what I've been looking for all along."

making your life count
(and Other Fun Things to Do with Your Time!)

the day started like any other day. My alarm rang at 8 A.M. I hit the SNOOZE for roughly four hours until it was noon. Time to rise and shine! Bleary-eyed, I searched my night-stand for my list of things to do that day. Immediately I checked off "get up" and proceeded to read through the rest of my tasks:

- Pick up socks at dry cleaners.
- Measure dental floss to determine how much is left on the roll.
- Mail ketchup rebate form.
- Special-order James Lipton bobblehead.
- Buy more paper to write lists on.

As I finished reading my list I suddenly felt sad and empty. *Maybe it's because you're hungry*, I told myself, but there was no response. (I'm not what you'd call a "morning person," so I don't always "answer" my own questions.) So I made my way down to the kitchen and whipped up some French toast and pancakes with a side of waffles. *Nope,* I thought after I'd finished eating, *I still feel empty.* The truth was I just couldn't stop thinking about my list and how all my daily errands only revolved around *me.*

I'd written nothing about saving the pygmy possum from extinction or setting up a feng shui institute for needy children in Suriname. It seemed I had completely forgotten to put "save the world" at the top of my list. And I didn't know if I still had time to do it.

Life is short. If you doubt me, ask a butterfly. Their average life span is a mere five to fourteen days. I headed out to my backyard in search of a butterfly who would have special insight into making the most of a short existence. I spotted a bright yellow variety that had alighted on my bougainvillea bush and introduced myself. "Hi, I'm Ellen DeGeneres. I live in the house back there. Boy, you sure are pretty. Could I ask you a few questions?"

"Yes," said the butterfly, nervously checking her watch, "but make it quick. There's a PBS documentary on water conservation that I want to catch." (It was a Swatch, by the way. A really teeny tiny Swatch. Those Swiss are design *geniuses*.)

"I've been thinking," I said hurriedly, "life goes by so fast. I feel like I haven't really contributed. How can life be made worthwhile in such a short amount of time?"

"I don't know what to tell you," said the butterfly impatiently. "I'm only three and a half days old and I've already volunteered my time to help a village in Bhutan increase its crop productivity by 80 percent. But you look like you've got a lot of life left in you. How old are you, if you don't mind me asking?"

"I'm forty-five." *(Note to reader: As you read this I might be younger or older than this, depending on whether you've recently traveled in a time machine.)*

"That's nothing," she said, preening. "Look at me! I'm middle-aged and I've never felt better. My doctor says if I keep eating right and cut down on my smoking I'll live for another four days! He's a great guy, met him when I was a day trader for three minutes last Tuesday."

"You were a day trader?" I asked in amazement.

"Oh, I've had many careers. Yesterday for about sixty seconds, I gave acting a try, but my agent barely sent me out on anything. I'm sure I don't have to tell you about the rampant ageism in Hollywood—"

"Uh, yeah, tough business," I interrupted, trying to get her back on track. "Please, tell me, what can I do to make my life count?"

She thought for a second—which for her must have been an eternity—and finally said, "Don't put off till tomorrow what you can do today." Then she took a peek at her wrist again (well, not actually her *wrist*, I guess, but I'm not up on my butterfly anatomy).

"Thanks for the great advice. I'll start tomorrow. Can I stop by and tell you how it's going?"

"I might not be here," she said, fluttering away. "Tomorrow I teach English as a second language in the Valley from 1:00:25 to 1:00:28."

"For only three seconds?!" I yelled up to the sky. But by that time she was gone.

Now, I don't want you to think that this butterfly in fact spoke with me. That would just be plain silly. Butterflies can't talk. (I'm not Dr. Ellen Doolittle, I'm Ellen DeGeneres.) The previous conversation was what I *thought* the butterfly might say *if* blessed with the power of speech. I say this because if I ever invite you to a dinner party, I wouldn't want you to bring your cat along as a date, thinking Snuffles might be a witty conversationalist. Just so we're all clear.

The next morning I got up early, grabbed my new list of five selfless tasks, and headed out to accomplish item number one: Walk an old lady across the street.

I live in L.A., where "old" means the wrong side of twenty-four, so I knew this one would be easy. I spotted an oldster listening to her iPod, waiting on a corner for the light to change. "Hello, ma'am, do you need help across the street?" I asked. For a moment the glare of her belly ring blinded me. I repeated the question and made an attempt to link her arm in mine. I must say, she seemed pretty agile for someone of advanced years—she ran very fast, skillfully dodging cars across all four lanes, and she kept on running when she reached the other side. Well, she *was* across the street, and whether directly or indirectly, I *had* helped. One down, four more to go.

Next on the agenda: Plant a tree. Frankly, I didn't have time to get a tree and plant it in some remote spot. Instead, I bought a few apples, took out the seeds, and scattered them in a Target parking lot à la Johnny Appleseed. One day, I hoped, the entire area would become the only apple orchard in the world with ample parking. With a flourish I checked off number two.

It was almost time for breakfast. A perfect time to "Conserve energy," which was number three on the list. It was about 100 degrees in incessantly sunny L.A. that day, "hot enough to fry an egg on the sidewalk," as my mother used to mutter under her breath, almost accusatorily. Of all the things she could "get on my case" about, as we used to say, I still can't believe she picked the weather, as opposed to, say, my huge bell-bottoms or my continual use of the phrase, "You're not the boss of me."

So, in order to get that pesky number three out of the way, I decided the best way to conserve was to harness the energy of the sun. If a bunch of drug-addled hippies could do it, why couldn't I? I cracked two eggs on the sidewalk and covered them in a light but tangy hollandaise sauce, then I waited. Hmm. Maybe it *wasn't* hot enough to use concrete as a stove top, as my mother had always led me to believe, but it *was* hot enough to jump in my car, turn on the air conditioner, and head over to Denny's.

Sitting in a cozy booth, I dug into my eggs Benedict and revised my goals. After deep contemplation, I came to the conclusion that using alternative energy in place of fossil-fuel energy was still, technically, using energy, not conserving it. So, to stay true to old "number three," I decided I would sit motionless in Denny's until they stopped refilling my root beer. After four hours (and thirty-seven trips to the bathroom), I realized that no energy conservation was taking place. I paid the bill (Two dollars and fourteen cents! How do those people stay open?!) and felt justified checking off number three. At least I hadn't mentioned anything about water conservation.

"Volunteer as a Big Sister" was item number four. Unfortunately, the day was almost over, so calling the Big Brothers Big Sisters of America was out of the question. Thinking quickly, I called up my ten-year-old neighbor, Abigail Van Splinter. Within minutes she knocked on the door, and I invited her in.

"Hi Abigail, I'm your big sister."

"No you're not."

"Yes, I *am*. Hey Abigail, do you want a 'Hertz Donut'?"

"Okay."

"I gave her a playfully hard punch on the arm. Hurts, don't it?"

"You're mean."

"I know you are, but what am I?"

"You're picking on me just like my real big sister. I don't need this. I'm going home!"

Man, that one was easy! Four down, only one to go.

Number five was a real doozy. To be honest, since I wasn't even quite sure where the Amazon rain forest was, singlehandedly revitalizing it was going to be a challenge. My knowledge of geography is limited primarily to where I've gone on tour. I couldn't recall performing stand-up in a rain forest, Amazonian or otherwise. Thinking quickly and quite geniusly, I turned number five into a big fat one. Then I put it on the top of my list for the next day.

I stopped to think about the things that I had accomplished and how much they would mean to the world. Maybe not today, maybe not tomorrow, but I knew that my medium-size contributions would really have an impact in the not-so-distant future. My ripple could already be felt as close as next door, with little Abigail waking up tomorrow morning with a sore arm and stronger resilience, and soon, as far away as however far away that rain forest on my list is.

That night I went to bed early, my list for the next day poised on my nightstand. But first, I made an important addition. Number two: Buy an atlas.

this is how we live

everyone likes to talk about how advancements in technology will change the way we live forever. Frankly, I think modern technology is hurting us. I really do.

If you want to know the truth, I blame the microwave for most of our problems. Anything that gets food that hot without fire is from the devil. If you don't believe me, put a Hot Pocket in your microwave for three or four minutes, then pop that thing in your mouth. If that's not Hell, my friend, I don't know what is.

Modern life requires hardly any physical activity. We just push a button and stand there. Take the car window. Someone decided that having to crank the window down yourself was too hard. "I don't want to churn butter, I just want fresh air!" So we got a button to do it.

We're just so lazy. We used to have breath mints. Now we have breath strips that just dissolve on our tongue. Can we not *suck* anymore?

Yes, we're lazy. Yet we also can't seem to sit still. So we've started making things like GO-GURT. That's yogurt for people on the go. Let me ask you, was there a big mobility problem with yogurt before? How time-consuming was it, really?

"Hello? . . . Oh, hi, Tom . . . Oh, I've been *dying* to see that movie . . . Umm, no . . . I just opened up some yogurt . . . Yeah, I'm in for the night . . . No, not even later—it's the kind with fruit on the bottom. Well, have fun. Thanks anyway."

And people are eating power bars all the time. Power bars were made for mountain-climbing expeditions and hiking, not really made to be eaten in the car on the way to the mall. Is it really that much faster and more convenient? It takes longer to chew one bite of those things than it takes to make an entire sandwich. I don't know what they're made from, but you could insulate a house with that stuff.

There are certain things that they're coming up with that I just don't think we need. Top of the list is that moving sidewalk you find in airports. It's like a little ride in the middle of nowhere, but I don't know what function it really serves. I mean, it's fun because it moves, so if you walk while you're on it you're almost like the Bionic Woman, just flying past the people trudging beside you on the ground. But you know how hard it is to adjust to walking again once you get off that thing? And what about those people who get on there and just stand? I guess we have to thank God they found the moving sidewalk. Without it, I don't know how they'd get anywhere.

You'd think with all these innovations that are speeding things up for us and moving us along, people would be early—or at least on time—when they're going places. But somehow, everybody's still always late. And people always say the same thing when they finally show up after you've been waiting for them. "Oh, sorry. Traffic." "Really? How do you think I got here? Helicoptered in? I *allow* for it."

How else does technology torture us? Well, try opening up a brand-new CD. What has happened to the packaging of CDs? These are angry, angry people, these CD packagers. "Open here," it says. Is that sarcasm? Are they mocking me? The plastic they use is so thick, it's like government plastic—civilians can't buy this stuff. And you can't get through it without slashing it with a knife or scissors or something. In fact, I find you need a sharp pair of scissors to get into just about anything these days. Have you tried to open a package of scissors lately? You need *scissors* to get into scissors. And what if you're buying scissors for the first time? I mean, how can you possibly get in there? Talk about a catch-22.

Batteries are also packaged as though the manufacturers never want you to get to them. What could possibly happen to batteries that they need to be packaged like that? On the other hand, take a good look at a package of lightbulbs. Thin, thin, thin cardboard that's open on both ends. What are *those* packagers thinking? "Oh, the lightbulbs? They'll be fine."

It's hard to get into anything, even toilet paper. What has happened to toilet paper in public bathrooms? It's not even one-ply anymore, is it? It's a sheer suggestion of toilet paper. It's an *innuendo*. It's like prosciutto, it's so thin. And if you're in a public bathroom and it's a brand-new roll that hasn't gotten started yet, just try to find the start of that toilet paper roll. First you turn it slowly. You think, *surely I've gone around once or twice by now.* Then you go fast. Maybe the wind will open up the first flap. Then you turn it the other way, thinking maybe you're going in the wrong direction. And back to the slow again. And then you find it, and it's glued down. So then you try to pull it apart but only a quarter of an inch separates and the rest stays glued. So you're pulling and pulling and soon you've got a five-foot-long quarter-of-an-inch strip. I don't want a streamer, I want toilet paper! So now one side is fully intact and you've got a groove cut out on the other side. Then you use your finger to try to even it out, but you never get it exactly even, so then you finally just claw at it like a wild animal. "Jesus, I just want toilet paper!"

On the other hand, some things that don't need to be made easier are being made easier. They're making these automated toilets that flush entirely on their own schedule. Sometimes they just go off randomly. You're still sitting down and suddenly it just flushes. "How *dare* you! I'll decide when I'm done!" And then other times it won't go off when you want it to. You stand up and stare at the toilet. Sometimes you have to fake it out. You sit back down . . . stand up! Sit down . . . stand up! Then you try tiptoeing away as if you're leaving. Nothing works.

Then, when you go to wash your hands, you don't have any control of that either. The faucet has to see your hands first so it can decide how much water it's going to give you. It gives out only a certain amount of water. You don't know how much you're getting, so you're like a little raccoon under there, rubbing your little paws together. It gives you some, then it decides *that's enough,* and it's not. So you have to pull out and pretend like you are a new set of hands going back in again. Same thing happens with the dryer—you don't have any control. You have to put your hands under the vent to get the air to come out. It's all to avoid germs, which is great, fantastic. Good for the health of the world. Then you walk over to that disease-ridden door handle, open it up, and head to the bowl of mixed nuts you're sharing at the bar.

Technology has done one beautiful thing for us. It's called the cell phone. There is now not one place in the world where a cell phone is not going off. And every cell phone now has its own little song! Good thing we got rid of those obnoxious rings, isn't it?

When you're on a cell phone, you can't ever have a full conversation. Usually the reception is terrible, and somehow it's only bad on your side. The person talking to you has no idea that you have bad reception. They're rambling on and on and you've got your finger jammed in your ear. You're shushing people on the street, ducking behind a Dumpster, putting your head between your knees, just so you can hear about your friend's new haircut. "What about the bangs? Are they shorter? Are the bangs shorter? THE BANGS!!"

At least if there's static you have some clue that you may get cut off. There's nothing worse than when you have crystal-clear reception and you've been rambling on for who knows how long, only to find out that the connection cut out who knows how long ago. Then you get paranoid. You're scared to talk too long ever again. Next time you're on the phone you become obsessed with checking. "So we were going to go to the cheese shop. . . . *Hello?* Okay . . . And we knew we were having white wine. . . . *Still there?* All right. And I thought, what kind of cheese would go with . . . ? *Did I lose you?* Okay . . . And I like Muenster. . . ."

Even if you're on a regular phone at home, you'll be interrupted somehow. You'll be interrupted by call-waiting most likely. Call-waiting was invented as a convenience, but let's face it—it's really turned into a mini People's Choice awards. You find out right away who wins or loses. You're having a pleasant conversation with someone you think is a good friend, and you hear the click, and you're confident that they're going to come back to you. Then they come back and say, "I've got to take this other call." And you know what that means. They just said to the other person, "Let me get rid of this other call." That's what you just became: a call to get rid of. Then you learn to trick them the next time, when they say they've got to check on the other call. "Hey, when you come back, remind me to tell you something that somebody said about you! . . . *Hello?*"

Of course, you don't have to pick up call-waiting. You can get voice mail. Voice mail will pick it up for you. My favorite voice mail is the one where you insert your name into a robotic message, and you end up sounding more like a robot than the robot itself. "Your call has been forwarded to an automatic voice message system. El-len is not available." Is that how I say my name? Like HAL from *2001: A Space Odyssey?* "Yeah, I'd like to make reservations for dinner tonight, there's four of us, and the name is El-len."

Phones have gone through such an evolution. Now we have this wireless technology that lets us talk to anybody, anywhere, anytime. Think about how far phones have come. You'll remember there was a time when there was one phone in the house, when cord was just being invented. There was a shortage of cord back then. Maybe you had a foot or two from the wall to the phone. Back then, when you said you were on the phone, you were *on the phone.*

Then the kitchen wall phone came along, usually a lovely mustard or an avocado green. It had a ninety-foot-long cord that allowed you to walk all around the house, clearing tables, wrapping around dogs, so that by the time you hung up the phone, it had become this tangled wire of cord confusion. But what was fun about it was that every once in a while you would hold the phone upside down by the cord and let that thing spin and spin, around and around, till it found its center. Good times.

One surefire sign that things are going the wrong way? Now we have the hands-free phone so you can concentrate on the thing you're really supposed to be doing. My thought is this: Chances are, if you need both of your hands to do something, your brain should be in on it too.

penny-pinching
for today's gal

or

How to Land a Man

The following is an article I was contracted to write for a major women's magazine several years ago. They thought I would be a good person to write a "helpful hints" type of column. For some reason, the magazine put a stop payment on my check after I turned in my first draft, and it was never printed. Just goes to show, some people aren't ready for true innovation!

hey, ladies, have you ever found yourself at a financial low, with no dough but someplace to go? Well, I'm here to tell you that you don't need money to make it happen; you just need a little creativity and a lot of spunk!

I've compiled the tricks and tips that I've used over the years to get past my empty wallet and get down to business—or even better, pleasure!

(Warning: The following tips were concocted and used in a time of crisis and may be dangerous to your health and/or pride.)

LOOKIN' GOOD

The key to having confidence about your appearance is all in the details.

Take your nails. Nothing builds self-esteem like a beautiful set of nails. Haven't had a manicure in a while or ever? Do it yourself by opening your car door and dragging your nails along the pavement whenever you slow down for a stop sign. Why spend money on emery boards when you can save dollars a year my way?

For a dramatic gray eye shadow and lash darkener use the ink that got all over your hands from that newspaper you found on the bus.

Haircuts are easy and fun, even for one! Especially with today's messy, just-out-of-bed styles, there's really no way to lose. If you can find a pair of scissors, you're in luck. All you have to do is bend over at the waist, grab the bottom part of whatever hair is in front of your face, and chop away. When you stand back up, not only will you have brand-new layers and no more split ends, but you'll also get a wicked head rush. Put the scissors down and enjoy.

If you can't find a pair of scissors, then a bread knife, an old razor blade, or a lighter are some options to consider. All these tools should be used with extra care, so drinking is absolutely not allowed while self-styling. Of course, when you're finished, it will probably be necessary.

If anyone criticizes you or says your new 'do looks bad, don't hesitate to inform them you just got back from Paris. Maybe it's lying, but what more do rude people deserve? Not the truth, that's for sure.

Speaking of which, one man's uneaten strawberry from the side of his daiquiri glass is another woman's free lipstick and blush. It's nature's perfect cosmetic. Just keep in mind, it's very sticky and you have to beware of bees, so apply it on a night you plan to stay indoors to reduce the risk of being swarmed. I made the mistake once of applying my "berry glow" in a 7-Eleven parking lot. One minute I was a beautiful strawberry juice princess, staring at my reflection in the rearview mirror, adding up how much I'd save by using fruit as make up every day for a year ($123.93) and the next minute, my head was covered in bees! Isn't Mother Nature a fickle, stinging prankster? That's why my personal motto is: "When life gives you lemons, use the juice to bleach your moustache."

FOOD IS RELATIVE

Everyone knows you can make a delicious meal by going to a restaurant, ordering a bowl of hot water and squirting packets of ketchup into it, thereby creating your own version of tomato soup. This is called "The Hobo's Delight," and there's no shame in enjoying it at even the finest eating establishments. Keep in mind, it's fat-free and ready-to-make!

Now, here's a modern spin on that classic 1950s recipe: Go to a high-class dining establishment of your choice. You may have noticed that people who eat at these places rarely finish what they order and almost never do if they find a bug or fly in their food. Take advantage of this tendency by going to your local novelty store, buying a plastic insect (you can get them real cheap if it's not close to Halloween), and placing it in their food so that they leave it untouched for you to swoop in on when they've stormed off in a huff. All you have to do is divert their attention before they start eating, maybe by saying, "Hey, is that a million-dollar bill on the ground by your foot?" They'll bend down because they're greedy and when they do, throw your plastic fly or spider or iguana or rubber garden snake or plastic flamingo or fake parrot or even a real parrot onto their plate. A real parrot would be the best because they're so loud and brightly colored, they're sure to offend anyone, but then again, you'd need a well-trained parrot and those parrot lessons can be very expensive, unless you know where to go. Luckily, I do, but that will have to wait until my next column. Anyway, no matter what pest you choose, you'll end up with a delicious entrée. *Bon appétit!*

And don't forget: You have the right to beverages! A lot of people don't know this, but in some states, you don't have to pay for your soft drinks if you tell the bartender you are your group's designated driver. This may be a problem, as you must have a "group" to drive in order to take advantage of this brilliant piece of legislation.

Keep in mind, most drunk people are relatively friendly, so sidle up to a couple of strangers talking at the bar, make sure the bartender can see you, wait until someone makes a joke, laugh as loud as you can, and then immediately order a Dr Pepper. It also wouldn't hurt to be constantly jangling your keys and saying things aloud like, "Yeah, suck 'em up, you guys. I've totally got this situation covered." Maybe for effect, slap one of the drinkers on the back in a friendly way, but get ready to run if they happen to notice.

HOME SWEET CAR

You can park overnight for free at a gas station by putting a note under your wiper that says you broke down and have gone for help. Usually, people break down and walk to a gas station, so this reversal of logic will baffle and bemuse the attendants. Be sure to tape newspaper up in your back windows so the attendants don't catch on that you're "camping out" in their "gasoline forest."

In the morning, wash your hair with hand soap and dry it with the hand dryer in the "patrons only" bathroom. If an employee confronts you and accuses you of not being a patron, refer him to your American flag bumper sticker and tell him that the flag is proof that no one is more patriotic than you. Immediately begin a rousing chorus of "This Land Is Your Land" and sneak away sometime during the first verse. (I suggest before "an endless skyway," which is usually the last line anyone knows for sure in that song.)

These, of course, are just a sampling of the many ways I've

found to cut corners. You can always come up with your own methods; all it takes is a little imagination and that old mother of invention, desperation!

And stay tuned . . . next week you'll learn how to make your own perfume out of rotten fruit (and, of course, where to get your free parrot lessons). Until then . . .

Helpfully hinting,
Ellen

working it out

dieting has to be one of the hardest things for a human being to do—that is, besides parallel parking. And unless you're a driving instructor or a valet, you know what I'm talking about. How many times have you found a spot on a crowded street and then, once you got ready to park, thought, "How am I supposed to fit this huge machine into that tiny rectangle of a space?" And then you remember, "That's right, I have to *back into it.*" What better way to do something you're already a little leery about doing than by doing it backwards? Meanwhile, cars are piling up behind you because they all want your space for themselves. You can actually feel their jealousy and impatience. The pressure is on. You check every mirror, turn all the way around in your seat, crank the wheel, step on the gas, and pray everything will work out. And most of the time it does, but only after you pull forward and back seventeen times so that you're not too far away from the sidewalk or too close to the cars in front of or behind you. It's precise, restrictive, and totally un-natural—just like dieting.

When you decide to go on a diet, it's never because you feel great and want to reward yourself by reducing your food intake and exercising more. The idea usually comes to you after you've gone bathing suit shopping or right before your high school re-union. You feel ugly, depressed, and totally unlovable. Let's face it: These are not healthy states of mind for a major lifestyle change. These are feelings that make you want to curl up with a quart of Häagen-Dazs and watch the Lifetime network all day.

Now, I'm not saying a made-for-TV movie starring Mered-ith Baxter doesn't have its own healing powers. (In fact, that woman has gotten me through some very rough times.) But if you're already down on yourself, lying on the couch watching reenactments of real-life heroism and eating as much ice cream as you can stomach is just a quick fix. Eventually, we all have to put the spoon down and get up off the couch.

When I'm feeling flabby, here's how I try to look at it: I've been on summer vacation with my body, and now it's time to get back to school! Everyone knows you can't learn anything at a school that has no teachers. This is why I recommend getting a personal trainer. Now, it sounds very "Hollywood" to have your own personal trainer, but, in fact, they have them at every gym anywhere in the country, maybe even the world, except Sweden. No one in Sweden goes to the gym. They're all tall and thin and healthy eaters by nature. It's something about the altitude and the fact that no starches are allowed in the country. I'm pretty sure I read that somewhere.

The good thing about personal trainers is that they make you feel guilty. Sure, that sounds bad, but think about it. How many times have you seen someone who jogs around your neighborhood every day without fail and thought to yourself, "How do they do it?" The answer is, they feel guilty enough on their own to *make* themselves do it. Sure, if you asked them, they'd say something like, "Oh, I love to jog." That's just ridiculous. No one loves to jog, it's painful and boring. People just feel like they have to. Getting a personal trainer is like buying that same guilty feeling, but with the extra bonus of disappointing someone besides yourself if you flake out. You practically *want* to work out. Practically.

I used to be the worst when it came to physical fitness, until my psychic introduced me to Rico, my personal trainer. We've been through a lot these past two years, but I'm all the healthier for it.

Not only did Rico guide me through the awkward beginning stages of my new fitness plan, but he also helped me with my poor-nutrition problems. I remember when I first told Rico that my weakness is coffee ice cream. You'd think I'd said I like to eat hundred-dollar bills.

"You can't eat that! Why would you want to eat that?"

This is the weirdest question I have ever been asked. I actually considered taking the time to explain to him why ice cream is so good. How could he not know? Then I remembered we were on my dime.

"It's delicious," I wheezed, trying to finish my fourth sit-up. (Trainers will always try to have deep, meaningful conversations with you while you're exercising. It gets your heart rate up.)

"Well, if you're gonna do that, you should have coffee frozen yogurt. It's half the fat and calories of ice cream." So I bought it and I tried it.

At our next session, I brought it up during my quad presses. "Hey, I had some of that coffee frozen yogurt. You know what else I could do instead of eating coffee ice cream? I could chew on a tan-colored towel." I thought I'd really got him on that one, but he just increased the weight on my quad press machine.

Rico was always giving me tips on how to lose weight faster.

"Drink more water," he'd say, doing sit-ups while hanging upside down.

"I do drink a lot of water," I'd reply. "Ice cream makes me thirsty."

These were the things I'd say to Rico to get him all riled up. He was hard to rile, though, especially when he was upside down.

Clearly, Rico had no understanding of my love of food. There are people who are like that. They don't really care about what they eat or when or how much or if they can get seconds. They just eat what's good for them. Who are these people?

Rico told me in all sincerity one day, "You can go to any

restaurant. Just don't order bread, potatoes, rice, fatty meats, dessert, or wine."

"Let's see, that leaves water and carrots. Sounds delicious."

I don't think he heard me. I was about fifteen feet away from him and had just caught the medicine ball he'd thrown to me. Well, *at* me. And hard—not the way a boy should throw to a girl. But that was Rico.

"You can eat whatever you want, just eat less of it. You like pizza?"

"Yeah! Let's go get some pizza!" I dropped the medicine ball and ran to get my jacket.

"No, I mean, if you like it you can have it. Just have one slice."

I don't think I've ever had just one slice of pizza. Unless it was one of those really big slices you buy one at a time. But those are easily three slices of regular pizza in one huge slice shape. I think the only way I could ever eat just one slice of pizza is if I had the one slice and then knocked myself out with a rock.

I wanted to quit. I wanted to go home. I wanted Meredith Baxter to take me away. Suddenly, I felt rage boil up in my belly. I felt the injustice of my genes. Why wasn't I born in Sweden like everyone else? Why did I need some jerk to stand next to me, counting my "reps" and telling me to feel the burn? I felt the burn all right and the burn made me want to punch my trainer in the face. And then, as if by magic, Rico appeared in front of me wearing headgear and holding up two large, red padded gloves.

"Are you ready for some kickboxing, baby?"
Oh, I was ready.

I have had many trainers since Rico, but I still miss him sometimes. If it weren't for him, I never would've gotten into kickboxing. And I'll always appreciate the fact that he didn't sue me. I did hit him pretty hard. Rico was a good sport. But what could he say to me? He was the one who got me so strong in the first place.

smartishness

do you feel insecure because you keep getting the nagging feeling that you're not that smart? Well, I've got good news for you, my friend. You have no need to be insecure. That nagging feeling is absolutely right on target. You are not that smart. But I have more good news for you. You are also not alone!

Let's face it: We're all stupid. Each and every one of us. Oh sure, some people went to college and got degrees—big whoop! I could have done that. I stayed in school plenty long. As long as the law said I had to.

You see, scientists have proven that we only use 10% of our brain. And that's on a good day. 10%! Let that figure roll around in your head a bit. You've got room enough—after all, you're only using 10% of it. It's just not that much, is it? I mean, imagine what we could accomplish if we used the other 60%.

Getting older doesn't help the ol' noggin either; let me tell you that. And I know I'm getting older because I just used the expression "ol' noggin." I'm not sure if it's happening to everyone, but I'm slower than I used to be. My mind is definitely slowing down. Maybe it's on a little vacation. Our brains need downtime just like our bodies. We sleep at night so our bodies can rest for a period. But our brains keep going with dreams. They never have a break. I would like my brain to cut down on the dreams and get back on the job for me during the day.

As I get older I'm losing my vocabulary too. It's not funny. I can't find words. Not even big words—just simple words. I'll start talking and I can't access a word I need. For instance, like . . . um . . . see, even now I can't think of the word. I'm not sure what's happening to me. It's like there's a Bermuda Triangle inside my brain, swallowing up all the words I've kept in there for forty-five years. Not that I spoke the first year, but I know I listened to words. I'm sure I absorbed things like, "She's wet again. You can change her." Or, "Boy, she's a fat baby. When's she gonna get some hair?" Or, "I sure hope she's got some talent 'cause she's not much to look at." Or, "That Studebaker sure is a good car. I'm investing all of our savings in *that* company."

"No, darling, let's leave it in asbestos."

"How 'bout we do half and half?"

"That's a great idea."

And I'm sure you've experienced this one: You know when you've forgotten what you're going to say even as it's coming out of your mouth? You're gabbing away to a friend, "Hey, you know what . . . ? What was I gonna say? What was I gonna say?" Now you're forcing your friend to participate somehow. "Um, we were talking about floor lamps?"

"No . . ."

"Mariah Carey?"

"No!"

Suddenly it's like you're playing *The $10,000 Pyramid*. "Uh, things that taste like chicken? Things a monkey would wear!"

"Yes!! That's right, we were talking about tiny hats."

It's terrible when you forget what you're going to say after two words, but what's worse than that, really, is forgetting what you're going to say when you've been talking for a while. You know, like when you're at a dinner party and a whole group of people are talking, discussing some heavy subject matter, and you don't really have an opinion on it. Then suddenly you think you do, so you jump right in there to share your opinion, and you realize you've actually got a pretty good opinion to share! When your friends hear this opinion, they're going to be blown away by how smart you are. They had no idea that you were so smart, and they will be shocked and impressed that you would come up with such an interesting point of view. And you start congratulating yourself, and suddenly, since you're feeling so good and you're celebrating too soon, you completely forget the point you were trying to make. And you're still talking. And they're looking at you like you don't know what you're talking about, and you don't, but you can't let them know that. So you just keep talking, praying that the point will come back to you. And not only does the point not come back, but now you've completely forgotten the subject everybody else was talking about. You really start sweating. You loosen your tie—if you're a man or Diane Keaton or Avril Lavigne—and then you try to jump out of it by saying any sort of generic statement that comes to mind. "Well, six of one, half dozen of the other. It's a slippery slope, my friend. Teach a man to fish. And, you know, there's no 'I' in team . . . Is there any more Merlot?"

I don't remember anything from school either. I don't know where Borneo is. Or South Dakota. I mean, I have a pretty good idea where it is in relation to North and East Dakota, but otherwise I'm lost. And I wouldn't know the difference between a sine and a cosine if they jumped in front of me naked in the middle of the street.

Here's all I remember of the Declaration of Independence: "When in the course of human events, bippity boppity boop." I have no idea what a conjunction is. I don't even know how I thought of the word "conjunction."

But even though I may not be book-learnin' smart, I still consider myself to be street smart (meaning, I think, that I usually know what street I'm on). And common sense–wise, I think I'm pretty smart too. Yet every single time I drive my Toyota Land Cruiser into an underground parking lot, I duck because the ceiling doesn't seem high enough and by ducking I'm helping my car make it. Plus, if by some chance we scrape the ceiling, my head will be protected.

Or let's say I'm walking out of my house, and I've just had a banana. I have my banana peel in one hand and my car keys in the other. I throw my car keys in the trash and walk out with my banana peel. The other day I found my iron in the freezer. And the only reason I found it is that I was looking for my sunglasses.

Sometimes I get a little down when I realize I'm never going to be as smart as I'd like to be. So I've come up with a few little tricks to make me feel better. You're welcome to try them out if you feel like it. I mean, you bought this book—you deserve that much. If, however, you're borrowing this book from a friend, I'd suggest you give your friend a few bucks first. Or, better yet, send me a few bucks.

One way, I find, to start feeling better about myself is to take a good look at really smart people I admire—people who have really accomplished something or seem to be extremely successful in the world. I really take a hard look at them, examine them. How did they do it? What do they have that I don't? What makes them so special? Who do they think they are? They're stupid! They think they're so cool. Well, they're not! And, presto, by making somebody look worse, magically you look better.

But even though the above method might make you look good to yourself, it's not going to do diddly (or P. Diddly, which I believe is the current expression) as far as the rest of the world sees you. For that, you need to be the next best thing to actually being smart. Which is, of course, pretending to be smart. How do you do that, you ask, scratching your head, a quizzical expression on your face, perhaps a long blade of grass between your teeth?

For one, big words make other people think you're smart. Remember, long words are better than short words, even if it's a bunch of short words. Here's a word you can use: kitchenette—it's a small kitchen. For instance, "Oh, you have such a nice small kitchen" is not nearly as impressive as "Oh, you've got a lovely kitchenette, don't you, now?" I added "don't you, now" to sound a little bit English. They all seem smart. If you can do a good English accent you don't even have to use long words. It's almost better not to—then you could just come off snobby.

Another way to appear smarter than you actually are is to have a few trivial facts at your disposal. Once you've memorized these facts, just sprinkle them into your ordinary conversation like . . . sprinkles, I guess. Here are a few that I use:

Telemachus—in Greek mythology, the son of Odysseus and Penelope, who helped his father kill Penelope's suitors. I'm not sure how you'll use this. So never mind.

Oh, how about *zwitterion*—in physics, an ion carrying both a positive and a negative charge, thus forming an electrically neutral molecule. Example: "Oh look, there's a zwitterion."

Albertus Seba was an apothecary. He was born in 1665 in the East Frisian town of Etzel. I have no idea what an apothecary is, or where the heck Frisia is. So, if I'm asked, I usually just point at something in the distance, then run in the opposite direction.

You can always try, "Alpacas communicate by humming and spitting." Then again, so does my grandmother.

And what if none of these methods work? What if you can no more pull off pretending to be smart than actually being smart? Well, there's no need to get depressed. Maybe smartness or smartyness or smartynessness just isn't for you. Which is okay, because if you look around, you'll see that people who are not smart have achieved success in every realm of endeavor. Look at politics; look at sports; look at who's on TV and in the movies. You're not going to see a lot of smarties. Look at me. I'm not all that smart and yet the accountant who I authorized to take care of all my finances told me that I made literally hundreds of dollars last year.

Feel better? Good. That's what I'm here for. Now, if you'll excuse me, I seem to only be using 8% of my brain right now. I'm going to go on a little expedition to look for the other 2%. If I'm not back in a couple of days, don't worry. Something shiny must have distracted me.

the things that are
bothering me this week

Last week in therapy, I was in the middle of a story when my therapist, Dr. Brandon Muflin, interrupted me. "Helen," he said.

"It's Ellen."

"Helen, Ellen, when you get down to it, is there really any difference?"

"Well, actually . . ."

"I don't want to get into your constant need to correct people. I've realized what your real problem is. You spend too much time in our sessions talking about yourself."

"But isn't that the point of therapy?"

"In fact, no."

Then Dr. Muflin (I know, don't certain people's names make you hungry?) suggested that instead of coming in each week and "yammering away" about the things that are bothering me, I should write them down—make a list of annoyances. He would then spend our therapy sessions reading my list while I did chores around his house. "Much like Daniel-san did for Mr. Miyagi in *The Karate Kid*," he added, trying to convince me.

Well, since Dr. Muflin's the one who is three credits shy of getting his B.A. from a partially accredited university, and not me, I decided to take his advice. So, without any further ado— okay, maybe with just a little ado—*ado,* here are:

THE 10 THINGS THAT ARE
BOTHERING ME THIS WEEK

1. Golden Delicious apples. Where do they get off naming their apples that? That's a little immodest, isn't it? What if I called myself "Incredibly Attractive Ellen"?

2. The way the receptionist at the dentist tries to book your next appointment six months in advance. "How's 8:45 A.M. on October the 5th?" I want to say, "Nope, that's no good. I'm shopping for groceries at 8:50 A.M. that day."

3. Businesses that offer to make up for poor service or poor products with a voucher for *more* free poor service or poor products. "If you're not satisfied with your meal, your next unsatisfying meal here is FREE!"

4. Car lot ads that brag, "Our sales manager screwed up! We've got too many cars and they must go. His mistake is your lucky break." How does this guy keep his job? Every year he screws up and orders too many cars. I don't want to buy from a dealership that allows this degree of incompetence.

5. The salesman at the big electronics store who tells you how well-made and dependable the TV is that he's trying to sell you, and that he's never had any customers who have experienced any problems with it. Then, when you get to the register, he tries to sell you the extended warranty.

6. My masseuse, who always says, "Boy, you're really tight today." Just once I'd like to hear her say, "Wow, your muscles are incredibly loose and relaxed. Why are you even here?"

7. When I'm standing at a cash register and the cashier says, "Ten twenty-five. Got a quarter?" I want to say, "No, I'm sorry. Let me find a cash register somewhere so I can get change and I'll be right back."

   OR, if I tell them I don't have the exact change, they say "No problem." I want to say, "I never thought there was a problem. You're the cashier. . . . This is a cash register. Making change is your job. I didn't expect a problem."

8. Bumper stickers that say, "I owe, I owe, so off to work I go." Or, "I'm late, but worth the wait." Okay, we get it. . . . You've got terrible money and time-management skills. These are character flaws. Why advertise them? While you're at it, how about, "I've got poor personal hygiene." Put that on a bumper sticker, why don't you?

9. The way ranch dressing is always ordered "on the side." It's the mistress of salad dressings. Won't somebody stand up and make a commitment to ranch dressing? Stop treating her like a whore. Let her come with the salad to the dinner party. Don't force her to drive in a separate car!

10. Dr. Muflin's blinds in his den. They're those metal ones instead of wood and they are almost impossible to clean. I know it's only his den, but you should never skimp on window treatments.

Well, I'd write more but I don't want to be late for therapy. My chores today are organizing Dr. Muflin's sock drawer, mulching his prize roses, and trimming the high branches in his apple orchard. Golden Delicious. It figures.

my dad was like a
father to me

i get a lot of cards and letters asking me to write about my dad. Well, most of them come from my dad. Sometimes he tries to fool me by signing a woman's name, then putting on lipstick and kissing the envelope. His scheme doesn't fool me. The return address sticker he got from donating to the ASPCA is a dead giveaway.

Since his birthday is coming up and I haven't found a good card yet, I figured I might as well give him his wish and write something about my dad.

I remember my childhood like it was yesterday or even this morning. Yet I was a little innocent girl, so I know it wasn't this morning because I was this age even yesterday. But what I remember most is late afternoon, dinnertime. Mama would be in the kitchen with Suky, our nanny. Suky was blind, so I don't even know why she'd be in the kitchen because she wasn't allowed to help cook. She once sprinkled the Christmas cookies with Ajax. I didn't mind. But anyway, if it was Friday, supper would be a big kettle of fresh vegetable soup. Grandma would chop the carrots and celery. Every week she'd wave her big cleaver in the air, calling out the same thing: "Ooh, this knife is sharp. Y'all be careful. Whoa! I can't control my arm! Just kiddin'." Grandma was so funny. And dangerous.

Usually, I'd be in the backyard playing *Starsky & Hutch* with my best friend, Lucy Tanzamar. (Hi, Lucy!) She had a huge head and always wore jumpsuits. My favorite was a bright yellow one with nuts all over it—every kind of nut, not just two or three. It had peanuts, pecans, pistachios, almonds, cashews, Brazil, acorns, macadamia, walnut, chestnut, pine, beechnut, filbert, hickory, mixed. Later we found out that peanuts, almonds, and walnuts weren't nuts at all but actually something called "drupes." We used to laugh about that, thinking, *Here we are knowing that, just little girls, and whoever designed that jumpsuit must've been an adult, but they didn't even know they made a huge mistake!* We wanted to write somebody but didn't know who to write. Anyway, I loved that jumpsuit.

When we heard my Dad's moped pull into the front yard, we'd get so excited. We'd run inside, where Mama would be making a big batch of banana daiquiris. We'd all be trying to guess what he'd be dressed up as. Every day it was different. Sometimes he'd be in a monkey suit, sometimes he'd be in pink fur, like a giant bunny. He passed out flyers for new businesses in the mall, so he got to keep all the suits. Sometimes, to sur-prise him, we'd all be in suits too: Mama would be a swordfish. Suky would be a mongoose. (We told her she was an alligator—she didn't know.) Grandma was an iguana, and so on. We'd light all the sparklers and dance around in circles, like elephants in a circus. Then my dad would enter and start juggling dishes while singing some Glen Campbell song. . . .

Whoa. Wait a minute. Okay, I'm so embarrassed. That's not my childhood, that's a play I saw in London. I'm sorry. I was wondering, because none of that sounded familiar. I'm think-ing, *Who's Lucy?* No, *my* childhood was totally different. I had a twin brother who was an albino Mexican midget and my dad sent us to a Swiss boarding school. No . . . that was a movie I saw. Okay, I've got it now. Obviously I've been trying to block it out, it was so painful. When I was eleven, my dad made me swim in a pool full of rats. No, wait, that was last week's *Fear Factor.*

Okay, I remember now. I look back on my childhood and I remember how my dad would play these practical jokes on me all the time. I remember one time so vividly. I was seven years old and I was in the backyard playing. Real hot, sunny day, about 97, 98 degrees, but not real humid. It was hot, though.

Anyway, I went into the kitchen to pour a glass of lemonade, because I used to just *love* lemonade. I still drink it. I don't drink it as much as I did when I was a little girl. Sometimes I'd drink it all day long. I'd drink so much that I'd be lying in bed at night, "Mom, I got a tummyache!"

Anyway, so I'm in the kitchen, and in the kitchen were my dad, my mom, all my brothers and sisters, just standing there, staring at me about to start laughing, and I'm like, "What?" So my dad said, "Ellen, honey, uh, we've never liked you as well as the other children. So, we've sold you to a tribe of Iroquois Indians. They'll be here to pick you up in about an hour. We're going to the Ice Capades. Good-bye! Good luck!" I was seven.

So, I lived in the Uriginees mountains for about nine years with the Iroquois, learning basket weaving and pottery making, and I taught them that noise you make under the armpit. That was the skill I had. And it was customary to marry within the tribe at thirteen and have several papooses, which I did. Cluck Cluck and Too Koo were their names.

Anyway, nine years later, trudging up the mountains came my dad, my mom, all my brothers and sisters, carrying a big pitcher of lemonade. Of course my tribe and I didn't recognize them—we were shooting them with bows and arrows and everything—but they got up to the top and said, "We're just kidding! We love 'ya! Come on home." And we went home and laughed, and laughed, and laughed.

Here's the funny thing. The funny thing is, they weren't even real Indians. They were actors my dad had hired to play Indians, just to fool me! Even today, I'll be watching an old rerun of *Love Boat* or *Mannix* with my dad, and we'll say, "Oh, hey, there's Running Steve!" That's not his real name; I know that now. It's Rick Schroeder! I thought he was an Indian! I didn't even know. He was always joking around, my dad.

My dad's famous saying was, "Kids, this is no picnic." Once he said it and we already had the tablecloth out on the grass and everything.

Actually, because my memory is so bad, most of that stuff about my dad isn't exactly, totally 100% true. But here's some stuff that is . . . kinda, a little bit.

My dad would always pay for things with change. I can see wanting to get rid of it; it's change. But if he was always paying for stuff with change, why was his dresser always covered with it? The entire top of it. I asked him about it one day and he said to me, "Beth, I'll tell you what, I've always loved coins. In fact, I wanted to be a pirate when I got out of college, but then I met your mother and before I knew it, I had a family to raise. I guess these coins are like the booty and this dresser is my treasure chest that will never be." I'm pretty sure he was just joking about not knowing my name.

When my dad would buy gas, he'd say to the attendant, "A dollar of regular, *Pahdnah.*" He called a lot of people "Pahdnah." I don't know if it was a New Orleans thing or if he just couldn't remember people's names. Come to think of it, he called me "Pahdnah" a lot. Not to mention that one dollar. But then to try to sound cool, he'd call the attendant "Pahdnah." I would slide down in my seat feeling sorry for the "Pahdnah." Don't know why he'd never spring for more than a dollar.

Of course back then (boy, that's when you know you're old, when you can say "back then"—you never hear a child say "back then") a dollar took you a lot further . . . farther? Let's just say it took you a long ways. We didn't have money really, but I didn't feel poor at all. That is, until we'd go out to buy something and my dad would pay for it with change. It's one thing to buy the newspaper or candy with change but a shirt or a lamp? That's not right. We'd be standing in line with him while he counted, "$34.50, $34.55, $34.60, $34.65. There you go, *Pahdnah.*"

Every Saturday and Sunday of my youth was spent looking at real estate that we couldn't afford. Not that these houses were mansions, which actually could have been fun. No, we looked at normal two-bedroom homes in regular middle class neighborhoods just out of our price range. That didn't stop my dad from looking at the same house over and over and over again. As a kid, I didn't really realize how completely insane this was. I was frustrated, though, because it was very exciting to think we could own our very own house. Every weekend when we would go back to look at it, I would imagine what it would be like to live there. Never mind that we were two children, grown, and these were two-bedroom houses.

There was always the same discussion at every house; "Well, your brother could sleep in the breakfast nook. Yes, a bed could fit in there. Or in the closet or garage." It would always end the same way. The house would be sold eventually and we would move on to the next one. I'm sure the real estate agents hated us. We must've been famous in the city of New Orleans for being "the family that looked every weekend for months at the same houses but wouldn't even make an offer." Actually, that seems unlikely because it takes so long to say; I doubt people would take the time to repeat it enough to make us famous. We were probably slightly well known.

We never owned a new car but we looked at quite a few. I remember being at a car dealership one time; I must have been around eleven years old. I was sitting in the passenger seat of a luxury sedan, flipping the vanity mirror up and down on the visor and wishing my dad's moped had a vanity mirror. Or even a passenger seat.

I looked over to see my father standing in the salesman's office, a sight I had never seen in all the time we'd spent wandering around every auto showroom in town. I looked around the big, beautiful new-car-smelling car that I was sitting in and dreamed of pulling up in front of my school in it, with everyone watching, even the substitute teachers. All the kids would ask me if they could have a ride; I'd say yes; and they'd hoist me onto their shoulders and parade me around the tetherball courts.

Right at the best part of this fantasy, the part where I was being awarded a lifetime supply of cafeteria Tater Tots, my father leaned into the car and said, "Let's get going, Bellhead." He called me that every once in a while when I was a child. I think it was his idea of a funny nickname, but it just made me think my head was really big. What did I know? I can't see my head the way an objective observer can. It took me years of therapy to realize that if my head could fit into a standard-size hat, it couldn't be much bigger than anyone else's. Thank God for that new school of psychology that developed hat therapy or I would've been convinced I was a bigheaded freak for the rest of my life.

Anyway, I asked my father what kind of car we were getting and if it could please be orange because that was the color car that I figured would make me most popular at school. He looked at me with a sweet, salty expression and said, "Oh, no, honey, I wasn't in there buying a car. The salesman and I just got to talking about how it's impossible to find a decent house in this city."

My disappointment must have gotten the better of me because I burst into tears. Come to think of it, I know it got the better of me because there was an unspoken ban on expressing emotion in our family, so I wouldn't have cried unless it was an absolute emergency. My father turned away until I was finished, then handed me one of his handkerchiefs with the little nose embroidered in the corner.

"Don't cry, Ellen. Someday you can write about this in your memoirs."

I looked up at my father, listening to the faint jingle of change in his pockets and seeing the love and kindness in his eyes and said, "You can't tell me what to do! You're not the boss of me!" Come to think of it, I was probably thirteen at the time. A wave of frustration had crested inside me and on that wave was the tiny, brave surfer of self-expression. I found myself "hanging ten" in a way I never dreamed I could before. I realized I liked that feeling.

Yes, thinking back, that outburst has come to symbolize for me the end of my childhood. After that, all my dad ever got from me was door slamming, curfew breaking, and the occasional eye roll, until I turned eighteen and left home to make it big on my own. I immediately gained thirty pounds just to prove I could, and for my efforts, my dad sent me a congratulatory Bundt cake with the words, "Keep it up, Darlene!" written in chocolate icing on top. I laughed and laughed, then I read the card he had so preciously tucked away in the empty center of the cake. It said,

Ellen,

　Be sure to have your laughs after you finish eating Bundt cake. It's thicker than you'd expect and can be dangerous if not eaten with caution, just like life.

Love,
Dad

the serious chapter

as a comedian, I've learned that people expect me to be funny all the time.

That is a lot of pressure, as you can imagine. I'm not the kind of person who is "on" all the time and I don't really like being around those types of personalities. It's draining to have to be their audience. I am funny but that doesn't mean I'm always funny. I'm also sad and mad and shy and serious. This is a chapter in which I can just be serious.

For some readers, it will be a chapter they skip over. "Why should we read a chapter that isn't funny," they might say. "I bought this book to laugh. I want to laugh at everything. What is this nonsense? I want my money back!" Well, calm down. I'll write one extra chapter, a bonus chapter, for those of you who feel ripped off. For others—the less demanding—this will be a welcome change of pace.

I've heard people say, "Why must everything be a joke with Ellen? Can't we learn a little bit about her as a person? Must she always be funny?" This chapter is for those people.

I hope that I've given you what you needed. I hope you feel complete in some way. I, myself, am bored.

the controversial chapter

after that last chapter, I find it necessary to give you something controversial. After all controversy sells. Or is it "sex sells"?
Well, in my next book maybe I'll do a sex chapter too. But for
now, let me be controversial. That is what I'm supposed to be. I
don't want to let anybody down. So here goes.

I hate puppies and kittens. That's right, you heard me. I
think they're stupid and ugly. And I won't pet them or play with
them, even if someone puts them on my lap. I find them repul-
sive and vile. Also, I abhor ice cream and I'm not even lactose
intolerant. I just refuse to acknowledge its significance in society. I also despise all things that are soft: Cotton? Yuck! Fleece?
Peeuuee!

Oh, and children's laughter is a turnoff to me. Children in

general are creeps, the color yellow is stupid, and I hate all green things, especially trees. Shrubs are okay, I guess. They're shorter, not as full of themselves. I dislike anything with pride or confidence. There, I've said it. If I've upset anybody, it's too bad. I don't care. I'm controversial! I'm a rebel!

the chapter of apologies

i didn't mean any of that. Who could not like puppies and kitties and ice cream and trees and soft things that are yellow? You would have to be a monster, a cold, heartless monster, born with no feelings! Wait a minute, I suppose it's good to have strong opinions and voice them. What's wrong with people expressing their opinions? We all should have that right. Freedom of speech! Freedom of expression! Obviously we can't all like the same things. That would be boring and it would create a nightmare for grocery shopping. Let's say everyone only liked vanilla ice cream, and that's the only flavor that was sold. We'd all be fighting over the last container of vanilla ice cream or they'd be out of it all the time. We'd all wear the same thing every day, like we were in Catholic school. We would be like robots, programmed to think and feel the way someone decided was the "right way." What is the "right way?" I like that we're all different. I want us to be different.

Me, I love cats, and I don't understand when people say they hate cats. I just think they've made a blanket judgment about all cats because they don't know a cat, or they met one bad cat with an attitude. I guess as long as people don't harm anything or anyone, they have the right to hate anything, but really, it's a shame to waste that kind of energy on hate. It's such a negative and draining emotion. Also, you're shutting yourself out of a possible opportunity to grow in some new area, to try to understand something that up until now you haven't understood. I'll tell you right now, I can't stand pepper—but I don't begrudge people putting it on their chicken. If they want to ruin a perfectly good *cordon bleu,* then let them.

You may still find you don't like cats (What's not to like?), but you don't have to hate them. You can say, "I don't understand cats, but I appreciate their existence." What I'd really like to express is, "I'm sorry." I'm sorry I pretended for three paragraphs in the last chapter that I disliked defenseless, beautiful, soft, and yellow things (which could be baby ducks).

So, in closing, I don't have a problem with controversy. I only wish the word we used was different.

dear diary

February 28, 2003

Dear Diary,

My thirty-five-city *Here and Now* stand-up tour starts in a week. I've decided that I should keep a journal to chronicle my adventures on the road. I tried to keep one on my last tour but I didn't have the discipline. Not this time. This time Diary, I vow to write in you every day, even though I have a huge problem finishing things I start. It seems to me that

March 3, 2003

Dear Diary,

I've been working out my act at a few clubs around Los Angeles. Last night went great. Of course, at this stage of the process I haven't memorized anything, so I'm still reading off notes I've written all over my hands. The audience didn't seem to mind. Even though I started out every joke with "Hands sure are funny, aren't they?" while staring intently at my palms . . .

March 7, 2003
Dear Diary,

I leave in two days, so I guess it's time for me to think about what I'm going to bring. When I'm on tour I usually travel with about fifteen steamer trunks. The hardest part is figuring out what I'll wear for each show. Should I wear a pair of pants? Or should I wear pants instead? I weigh the options. Pants? Or pants? Then I realize I'm usually most comfortable onstage in pants. Still, bringing along some pants is probably a good idea. Just in case I change my mind . . .

March 8, 2003
Dear Diary,

I'm going to stop writing "Dear Diary" at the beginning of each entry. There's no need for it. I'm just writing to myself. I suppose I could begin with "Dear Ellen," but then it would be as if I've got a second personality with the same name and personality as my main personality. Anyway, spent most of my day working on my act. Getting my material just right for an audience takes a lot of serious preparation, so I practiced my routine in front of my cats. They always have pages and pages of notes for me. The critiques usually focus on why there aren't more jokes about cats in my act. Why don't I have a "Phone Call to a Cat" joke or a "What if Gloria Estefan Was a Cat" bit? I try to explain to them that my audience does not usually consist of cats, but they feel that I'm limiting myself. Maybe they're right. You know what they say about a cat's intuition . . . or is it the nine lives of a good woman?

I've also decided to learn about each city I'm visiting on my tour. It's so important to connect with the crowds at my shows. When I take the stage I want to say more than just: "It's great to be here in (insert your city here)!" With the intensive research I've been doing, I'll be able to open with: "Hello, Kansas City! Did you know that your annual relative humidity is 60%? You guys ROCK!!"

March 9—Luther Burbank Center, Santa Rosa, Calif.

Well, I've finally hit the road. I just finished up two shows in Santa Rosa, California. Both performances were sold out! I was so excited when I heard. I was afraid I was going to have to take a bullhorn to the mall and give the tickets away. Since I didn't have to, I had more time to shower and change before the show.

Speaking of which, my act is really starting to take shape. The best part was that the audience was definitely laughing *with* me and not *at* me. Like the time I performed with my oxford shirt on backwards by mistake. You'd think someone would have told me before I went on.

The staff at Luther Burbank Center was so accommodating. The theater had a very nice greenroom. "Greenroom" is a fancy showbiz term for a backstage waiting area. It's not actually green. But no one dares ever mention that. Not if they want to keep their jobs. The room was appointed with my few simple requirements: just a big bathroom, a comfy couch, and a kiln, in case I want to calm my preshow jitters by fashioning an urn.

March 11—Capitol Theatre, Yakima, Wash.

I was a little nervous about performing in Yakima. It's a pretty small town. Very quaint. I didn't know if they'd accept a city girl like me, coming in with all my fancy city ways—my highlighted hair, my constant use of the word "barista," my subway tokens. I couldn't have been more wrong. The people of Yakima ("Yakimites," as I now call them) were so warm and kind and polite. And they love to laugh. I'm now putting Yakima on my list of top ten favorite cities along with Paris and Rome.

March 14—Kansas City, Mo.

Arrived in Kansas City late last night. Checked in to my hotel under my usual alias, "Nelle Sereneged," but the hotel clerk wasn't fooled by my little charade. He said, "But Miss De-Generes, that's just your name backwards." With my cover blown, I hastily checked in as Gwyneth Paltrow, only to notice Gwyneth waiting to check in right behind me. What are the odds?!

March 18—Grand Junction and Colorado Springs, Colo.

I loved performing at Kansas City's Midland Theater, a beautiful old building built in 1927. Sammy Davis Jr. and

Dolly Parton have played there, so I guess it was only a matter of time before I did. As a performer, I've always felt I was the perfect mixture of those two, with a dash of Carol Channing for zest. Then it was on to Grand Junction, Colorado, and Colorado Springs. Both shows were a delight.

Have I mentioned my opening act? Karen Kilgariff is the head writer for my new talk show and she's been traveling with me for the entire tour. She's been doing an amazing job warming up the crowds. Having a warm-up act is kind of like having your own personal food taster. Karen bravely goes out there to see if the crowd is good; that is, if they "taste" good to her. Some audiences of course are an acquired taste, but if Karen thinks the audience is "poison" (meaning sleepy and unresponsive), I don't go on. Instead, I am whisked out the back door to the safety of a cozy neighborhood bistro. . . .

March 19—Colorado to Seattle

I'm writing this as we drive through the frozen tundra of Colorado toward an airport that might be open so I can get to Seattle for a 7:30 show. There was a huge snowstorm; most of the roads are closed. We've been driving in the storm for two hours and have a couple more to go. We're all hungry, but there is not one store or restaurant open. In a desperate attempt to eat, I tried ordering room service, but realized that our hotel would have to airlift the food to our car.

The Denver show was canceled because no one could get to the theater in the blizzard. I'll be back in Denver March 26.

Hopefully the weather will cooperate. Getting to the show was no problem for me. My hotel was right across the street, but I guess other people live farther away. To pass the time during the storm, Karen and I have been gambling, playing cards, and pool hustling—all at once. It's been causing great confusion and consequently we're making a killing.

Actually, I heard that a few expeditions did try to make the trek to the Denver show, but most had to turn back. A five-person team from Argentina had trained for six grueling months for the event. They say their spirits were not broken and they vow to make it to the rescheduled March 26 show.

So here we are driving along, Karen, my assistant, my tour manager, and Lewis, my choreographer. We've got to make it to Seattle! Of course since we're all from L.A., where a cold snap means high 60s, none of us has warm enough clothes on.

I'm kicking myself for wearing my favorite travel sarong, and I know Karen is questioning her tube top choice.

I'm getting a little concerned. I see cars on the side of the road abandoned by their owners. If we break down, I have a backup plan to go by sled. I've been systematically collecting animals along the way to assemble a "team." So far we've picked up one squirrel, two dogs, and something that could be a hedgehog or a possum. I'm not sure. But if he can pull, he's in. If the sled idea doesn't pan out, I don't know what we're going to do. I don't know how to build an igloo or prepare whale blubber.

Later that night, at the Paramount Theatre in Seattle

We made it in the nick of time. After using several modes of transportation, including a car, plane, and finally a collapsible canoe (that wisely I had packed just in case), we arrived safely in Seattle. It was all so worth it. The Seattle show went so incredibly well that I've become giddy. I love the people of Seattle, every single one of them. But I especially adore the people that came to my show tonight. Being onstage and making people laugh is really an amazing feeling. I wish I could explain it. I wish I could book all my fans into select venues across the country so they'd know what it's like.

I've just been informed that we're heading out to the Great White North after spending about four hours in Seattle. The only sightseeing I got to do was reading a brochure for a Space Needle tour. It sure looks neat.

March 21—Orpheum Theatre, Vancouver, B.C.

I was very excited to perform in Canada again. It's like a whole different country! Learning about new cultures is so interesting. It's very important when visiting other countries to at least try to speak their language. During my set I made sure to pronounce "about" as "aboot." It's the key to winning over Canadian audiences.

Went to dinner after the show and sampled one of Canada's local specialties: Funions. At least that's what they told us.

March 22—Schnitzer Concert Hall, Portland ,Ore.

Well, I'm back in the United States of America, in a beautiful city called Portland. It's taken a bit of getting used to, after my whirlwind international experience.

I've been on the road for almost two weeks now. I miss my animals. I wanted to bring them along, but then my "posse" would include mostly cats and dogs. I think a posse is considered cooler if it's primarily people. Gotta wrap this up; we head out to San Francisco in the morning and I'm going to need about twelve hours of sleep so I can make it up those hills.

March 24—Davies Symphony Hall, San Francisco, Calif.

I always love visiting San Francisco. I lived here so long ago, when I was just a penniless stand-up comic just starting my career.

I took a cable car to see where I used to live. It's amazing, as you get older, how much smaller everything seems. Turns out, my old apartment was actually a galvanized steel garden shed (8'W x 3'D x 5 1/2'H) from Sears. I've come such a long way. For lunch I ate all the famous local foods, all at once. RICE-A-RONI (the San Francisco treat), Ghirardelli chocolate, sourdough bread, and a refreshing glass of wheatgrass juice.

Afterward, I felt a little queasy, so I clipped on my safety rope and made the steep ascent back to my hotel.

Davies Symphony Hall is a perfect place for comedy, because symphonies are always so damn funny. I came prepared.

In case the crowd demanded a tune, I brought my autoharp on-stage with me.

March 30—Majestic Theatre, Dallas, Tex.

It's my last night in the Lone Star State. You know, what they say about Texas is true. Everything is bigger. The food portions, the hats, the bed-linen thread counts. Remember that TV show *Walker, Texas Ranger?* That was HUGE. I rest my case.

Okay, here's more proof that everything's bigger in Texas. You know those teeny tiny miniature shampoo bottles you get in hotels? In Texas they come in five-gallon jugs—which makes stealing them a logistical nightmare.

April 2—Dodge Theatre, Phoenix, Ariz.

Each night, at the end of the show, I've been doing a little Q & A session with the audience. It's fun, and since I've been talking nonstop, it's nice to give somebody else a chance. The people's questions range from wanting to know the status of my latest projects to their asking me to define the molecular structure of certain kinds of cheese. Not all the questions are ones I can answer. But I always try.

April 4–6—Wiltern Theatre, Los Angeles

The Wiltern Theatre is incredibly beautiful. It was originally called the Historic Wiltern Theatre when it was built in 1931. Now it's just called the Wiltern Theatre, without the "Historic."

Why would they have called a building that was just built "historic," anyway? Would you call a brand-new restaurant Ye Olde T.G.I. Friday's? I think not.

April 10—Palace Theatre, Columbus, Ohio

Had a splendid show at the Palace Theatre and then back to my hotel room to get some rest. I am getting so used to living in hotels now. They're like a second home to me. I'm trying to organize a block party on my floor, but so far no one has responded to my flyer. . . .

April 15—Tower Theatre, Philadelphia, Pa.

Do you know how long it's been since I've had a home-cooked meal? When you're on the road you eat every meal out. Every one. All I want to do is make myself a tuna melt and eat it standing up in my kitchen. I almost never order room service when I'm touring because it's hard to justify eating a $10 boiled egg.

April 20—Symphony Hall, Atlanta, Ga.

It's so nice to be back in the South, back on familiar turf. Atlanta is one of the friendliest towns around. Everything is "yes ma'am" and "no ma'am." My favorite is "y'all" (which I still use). It's such an economical way to talk. "Y'all goin'?" is so much easier to say than, "Are you presently considering departing?"

Went to a Krispy Kreme donuts. The woman behind the counter was amazingly pleasant. In L.A. if you go into a store it's never like that. At the end of a purchase you say, "Thank you for letting me shop in your store." To which the shop person usually replies, with a shrug, "Whatever."

April 26—Massey Hall, Toronto, Ont.

Well, back on the plane again. Being in a different city every night is getting kinda wearing. So much packing and unpacking. By the time I've put everything away it's time to pack it back up and go.

I do make sure to keep each room I stay in neat and tidy. The whole "trashing" thing isn't really my style. Instead I like to leave a little something behind to make the room just a bit nicer. Sometimes I leave a houseplant. Or, as I did in my hotel in Toronto, I repainted the bathroom. I chose a charming French Blue, which I then "ragged" over with a vibrant Sunburst Yellow. I sure hope the hotel management appreciates it.

April 27—Benedum Center, Pittsburgh, Pa.

I've been on the road now for almost two full months and today I finally got around to writing some postcards. Now if I just had time to get stamps . . . Maybe I'll get them when I'm back in Los Angeles.

I wanted to see the Andy Warhol Museum (he was born in Pittsburgh) but didn't have time, so I just popped into a local supermarket and contemplated the Campbell's Soup section. It was the best I could do.

April 28—State Theatre, New Brunswick, N.J.

The show was sold out—what a great night! Next stop is New York City to tape my HBO special at the Beacon Theatre.

The next time I write I'll be in NYC, "the city that never sleeps." I'm a tiny bit concerned because I don't want my audience to be sleepy. I need them to be alert and on top of their game. I hope New York takes a nap before my show.

May 1–2—Beacon Theatre, New York, N.Y.

Just finished taping the show for HBO at the Beacon Theatre. Before the show I had a meeting with the director from HBO. The man has incredible insight into his craft. When I asked him, "What's my motivation?" he thought for a moment and then responded simply, but with great conviction, "Be funny." Let me tell you, those are two powerfully inspiring words. Well, actually his complete answer was, "Look, I don't have time for this. It's a stand-up show, right? Just be funny, for God's sake." But I knew what he meant.

May 5, 2003

I'm finally home! The tour is over and the HBO show is "in the can." It's hard to adjust to being in my own house after living in hotel rooms for so long. When I dial "zero" on my phone to tell the front desk that I need more towels they hang up on me. It's weird. Anyway, I don't think I'm going to tour again for a long, long time. Not unless I can beam myself to the various destinations. When some sort of transporter device has been invented, tested, and sold to the public, I'll go on tour again.

I'm thinking maybe early spring 2086.

a scientific treatise regarding
a matter of great entomological
concern to all of us

Whaat is it with bees?

it's just an expression

the other day I had an epiphany while eating a bag of potato chips. The bag was so full of air, I had to burst it like a balloon to get it open, and inside were only five or six measly freeze-dried spud slivers. It got me thinking how people fill conversations with trite expressions and phrases, creating the illusion they've said something significant, just like a deceptively puffed-up bag of chips.

Well, not really. What actually occurred to me was that snack food is a huge rip-off, but that's beside the point.

My point is . . . and I do have one (which, by the way, was the name of my last book—if you haven't read it, you really should, but please finish this one first) is that we no longer say what we mean or mean what we say. Do we honestly think that interjecting "Every dog has its day" or replying with "Is that so?"

contributes to the conversation? No, all it does is prolong the meeting, party, or intervention, cutting into time that could be better spent at home zoning out in front of the television.

Take this overused phrase: "Honesty is the best policy." Is it? Honesty is good, yes, but not always. Up to a certain point you should be honest, but just imagine if we were all honest all the time. The world would be terrible. It would be a cold, cruel place.

"Gosh, Sarah. Have you gained a lot of weight, or what? You're so puffy."

"Boy oh boy, that breath of yours is something else. I'm about to pass out. Seriously, that has to be the worst breath ever."

"Has your ass always been that flat or am I just noticing it now for the first time?"

I'll tell you what's really bad—going up to your friend whom you haven't seen in a while and saying, "Oh my God, you're pregnant!" and they're not. I've done that, and I'll tell you—the look on his face! He looked at me blankly and said, "As far as I know, men can't have babies."

I tried to cover, but it was no use. "Oh, I thought I read somewhere they can."

How many people can honestly say they're completely honest? Not too many. That's why people have to put their hand on a Bible and take an oath to testify in court. Everyone just assumes that people lie. We have to say "I swear to God" or "I swear on my mother's life, may God strike me dead!" if we really want to be believed.

I really never lie. I don't—I swear to God. (Like you have to—like God doesn't know the truth!) I must admit, though, I do lie to my Lifecycle. I lie right to its control panel. It says, "Enter program/fitness." I push ENTER. Then it says "age" and I punch in "35," and I push ENTER. I don't want the machine to give me a workout for a forty-five-year-old.

We want to believe people are being honest when they announce, "I have something important to say." I know I do, because I use it as a cue to turn on my hidden tape recorder. It's quite a clever ruse, actually, because if instead they told the truth and declared, "I have something to say that's so dull, so tedious, it'll make you wish you didn't have ears," who'd listen?

When it comes to clear communication, these useless phrases, expressions, and clichés aren't really up to snuff. Whatever that means. Let's just say that people say a lot of things that are ridiculous.

For some reason, when people try to cheer you up or point out that things could be worse, they say all sorts of stupid stuff. This is one somebody told me: "I felt sorry for myself because I had no shoes, until I met a man with no feet." Um, okay, what do you say to that? Yes, it's terrible he has no feet, but that doesn't change the fact that the other guy doesn't have any shoes and the guy with no feet doesn't need shoes. The guy with feet does. I mean, are we supposed to feel sorry for the guy with no feet? Because I'll tell you, I saw a guy on TV who only had a torso. Didn't even have a head.

And how about theses doozies?

1. What doesn't kill you makes you stronger.
2. Adversity builds character.
3. God doesn't give you anything you can't handle.

I've revised those sayings to make them more accurate:

1. What doesn't kill you puts you in a whole lot of pain and makes you cry a lot and want to crawl into a hole forever and live with rodents.
2. Adversity builds character. Translation: You become bitter and angry and then people hate you even more.
3. God doesn't give you anything you can't handle . . . unless God's in on it and doesn't like you either.

It comes down to the fact that people love to talk. Heck, I've made a career out of it. We delight in the sound of our own voices—especially those cheerful voices that yell out "Careful!" right after you stumble. If those people were truly looking out for us, wouldn't they have said "careful" *before* we tripped? A warning like that is as pointless as a photographer telling a pair of newlyweds that they both have spinach in their teeth immediately *after* taking their picture. Yes, Alanis, that's *way* worse than rain on your wedding day.

What's even worse is the new trend of saying "Ya know what I mean?" Often, people say it after each and every sentence. "Ya know what I mean?" It's used so much it's become one word: "YaknowwhatImean?" People who use it seem unsure if they're being understood correctly. I admire that. I always repeat back what they have said to ensure I've comprehended.

"Now, what I *think* you're saying is that you're thirsty, but I'm only saying that because you just said you *were* thirsty, but I might have misinterpreted. You could've been cryptically explaining to me the genetic code of the common housefly, and if that's the case, no, Idon'tknowwhatyamean.

Verbal padding is everywhere, but my biggest pet peeve is when someone asks, "Can I ask you a question?" Okay, first of all, that *was* a question. Do you want to ask me *another* question? This will be your second, and that's my question limit, so make it a good one. You can waste even more time and money (yes, time *is* money) by responding with, "That depends on what the question is." Now, let's do the math here. (Remember, one minute of personal time can be worth up to 75 cents!) "Can I ask you a question?" How would you know if it's the kind of question you'd care to answer unless you actually heard it? You can't. Anyway, it's not like you're at a press conference. . . .

"I'm sorry, I can't answer that question at the present time."

"But all I asked was, 'Do you know the way to San Jose?' "

"I'm sorry, but unless you're Dionne Warwick I have no response."

"But I *am* Dionne Warwick!"

And so it goes. . . .

So for the good of all humankind I suggest that we liberate ourselves from these empty expressions and wasted words. For your
reference, here's an incomplete list of phrases I kindly ask that
nobody say around me anymore:

"Stop and smell the roses."

Well, what if you're allergic to roses?

"Wake up and smell the coffee."

What if you drink tea? What then, Einstein?

"Happy as a clam"

Okay, if clams are so happy, then why do people "clam up"
when they get mad?

"Heaven's to Betsy;" "For the love of Pete"

Who is Pete? Who is Betsy? Do they know each other?

"Take care."

"Take care" is short for "take care of yourself." What does
"take care" mean? Where's the care? I'll take it. Pretty soon it'll
be just "take." Maybe that's what the British are doing with "ta-
ta." It's short for "take care"—"ta-ta." Or maybe it's some sort of
potato dish. I don't know much about the British, I just know

they enjoy wearing hats and trench coats and eating boiled meats.

"Have a nice day."

Cashiers and other service-industry people are forced by their supervisors to say this to every customer. The cashiers don't mean it. What they're really saying is, "Please, God, I don't want to get fired."

"He (or she) wouldn't hurt a fly."

Everyone hurts flies. Someone realized the hatred of flies is so universal that they actually came up with a device to kill them. They tried to disguise it with a nice gentle name: a "fly swatter." No, it's a fly *squasher.* Nobody buys it just to swat at them playfully.

"Well, I'll be a monkey's uncle."

Aren't families dysfunctional enough as it is without bringing innocent animals into the picture?

"The sun'll come out tomorrow."

Yes, but only if you're the one who wrote the song of the same name for the hit musical *Annie.* In that case, the sun comes out for you every time you receive your big fat royalty check.

"Nothing is forever."

However, diamonds apparently *are* forever. They also happen to be a girl's best friend. Man's best friend? The much less flashy *dog*.

"You win some, you lose some."

Although, I do have the habit of saying this one during sex.

"That J. Lo is a hot little number!"

(I know that's not technically an expression, but my mom said it once and I'd prefer she never say it again.)

Well, that's "the long and the short of it."

See what I've done here? I've wasted your time by using that phrase: "the long and the short of it." If I've included it as a way to quickly wrap up this chapter I've defeated the purpose. Not to mention the words I'm now using to explain this to you. (So far 56, plus the words in these parentheses, which brings us to a grand total of 76, but who's counting?) On top of that, I haven't made any sense. How can something be long and short? It can't. It's physically impossible. You can't be fat AND skinny or hot AND cold or ugly AND pretty. In the seventies, my mother did have some orange shag carpet that was pretty ugly, but that's a whole 'nother can of worms.

clothes i have regretted wearing

My mother called me the other day while she was cleaning out the clutter in her house. She said, "Ellen, I'm making room for my bowling trophies and I need you to come get some of your old stuff. I've boxed up your model horses, rock polisher, Hot Wheels, eight tracks, scrapbooks, and clothes. I need you to come get them. They'll bring back some nice memories— Oh look, I see your old sailor top in here."

Yes, it's true, I had a wool sailor top—you know, the dress blues—that I would wear all the time. I had a white one too. I wore that one when I went on leave. No, I wasn't in the Navy. I just liked uniforms. When I look back on the stuff I used to wear, I wonder why somebody didn't try to stop me. Just a friendly warning, "You *may* regret this," would have been fine.

I picked up at least a dozen boxes from my mother's house. I don't remember owning enough bolo ties to fill a box, but apparently I did. And piles of pictures—rolls and rolls of photos. It's one thing to touch and feel a polyester blend blouse, but to see a photo of me actually wearing it—proof, if you will—was inexplicably more disturbing.

I'm sure the Bee Gees look back fondly on their black poly/rayon/fire hazard shirts and think, "Oh, yeah, this is when we became millionaires." But when I look at my wearable fire hazard, my thoughts aren't as glamorous—they entail a desk job at Hertz and wine coolers at Doc McGee's Crab Hut. That was the one fantastic thing about those shirts: They went from day to evening, which is always a fashion plus. Who wants to go home and change, thereby increasing their chances of missing happy hour?

Why did I save all those clothes? I felt like that guy with amnesia from *Memento*. I'd pick up a pair of stirrup pants and an image would flash into my head: me standing in front of a mirror thinking, *These are really slimming*. Then all memories of that outfit and time would disappear.

I started combing the photo albums, mesmerized by this girl who was in no shape or form the person I am today. Lots of shots of me and pleats. Me wearing pleats, me enjoying pleats. Pants, jackets . . . Pleats on jackets? That's clearly wrong. Yet I thought they looked great. In one picture I am standing with this woman I worked with and we are both wearing what looks like trousers from a zoot suit. I added a backwards snap cap. Plus, the top of a Navy uniform. Were we on the lam? Maybe on the way to an audition for *Breakin' 2: Electric Boogaloo?* It didn't even look like me.

Several other photos revealed me wearing a series of paisley vests. In one I had a watch in the pocket. Let me just say that one more time. I had a pocket with a watch in it. I had a pocket watch. Apparently I waited for trains a lot. That's the only reason I can think of for needing a watch in my pocket. On the other hand, that's really all those vest pockets were good for; maybe I thought it was a shame to let them go to waste. Either that or I used to be a hypnotist.

It started to occur to me, if I'm horrified and possibly scarred for life after looking at these pictures now, in twenty years will I look back in shock on the clothes that were in my closet today? Will I think, *Why in the world would I wear Puma running shoes with dirty denim cargo pants?* No, of course not. That is a perfectly timeless outfit. In fact, it's retro. It's back for a second round. Maybe that's why I saved all those clothes at my mother's place—just in case they made a comeback.

I pulled out some painter's pants. I don't think they're back yet, but they reminded me I need to paint the hallway. There were lots of thrift store men's blazers too. I checked the pockets and found a ticket stub to an Elvis Costello concert—his glasses are still in, but not the jacket.

How do people decide what's back? More important, how do people decide what's never coming back or what clothing is over? For instance, unless you were going to dance class, when did it become not okay to leave your house with jazz shoes on?

Obviously, when the time came, the upper fashion echelon signed a bill—or proclaimed a style exodus, or sent out carrier pigeons, or maybe they just phoned each other, I don't know—saying a decision had been made regarding bolero jackets or parachute pants, and that they were never to be worn again.

How do the average people of the world receive this message, this change in the fashion tide? I don't recall anybody ever telling me, "You need to take off that zipper shirt and put one on with the neck and sleeves cut off of it. Immediately! They're watching!"

It was always kind of a slow metamorphosis for me. I'd find myself walking around and noticing nobody was wearing the things I had on or had hanging in my closet. I'm sure people were secretly pointing at me.

"Look how high her shoulders are."

"Her buttons are huge!"

"What, is she going to lift weights with that wide belt on?"

"I guess she didn't get the newsletter."

As I sifted through the pictures, I found that the older I got the less my clothes stood out. Then I looked down at what I was wearing that moment: a long-sleeve T-shirt and a pair of 501s, an outfit that has been around since the Gold Rush. Yet I wasn't wearing this or a variation of these timeless pieces in any of the photos, and I know I have owned them at every stage of my life. Maybe subconsciously I only had my picture taken when I was wearing something that would later embarrass me. Or maybe I thought, *Hey this is a great outfit—I'd better document it for a future retrospective. The world will want to see.* Just like the Jackie O exhibit at the Metropolitan Museum last year. A museum showing one woman's wardrobe. Hmm. Turns out she didn't wear a lot of bolo ties.

I boxed up my clothes, prepared to give them to Goodwill, and then thought, *In ten years I might want to look at these again*—not with regret, but with confidence that the clothes I will be wearing then could just as well be the clothes I wear now—only dirtier and with more pockets.

naming my book:
the odyssey

The funny thing is, to fully understand how and why I chose the title *The Funny Thing Is . . .* for my book, we need to go back in history. Remember the year "Billy, Don't Be a Hero" was a huge Top 40 hit? Well, luckily we have to go back much, much further—all the way, in fact, to 1454 or 1620 or the early or late fifteenth or seventeenth century. I can't really say for sure because I'm getting all of this secondhand.

Anyway, sometime, a real long time ago (about a decade before the introduction of books on tape), the Bible became the first book published for the masses. Who knew this amazing achievement would one day result in books with such titles as *Men Are from Mars, Women Are from Venus* and *Jesus for Dummies.* Yes, it's been a long, strange journey.

Over the years, as more books were published, it became

necessary to name them. Today, just as in 1454, if you stroll into a Barnes & Noble you need to know the title of a book in order to find it. I wanted to be sure, so I decided to test my theory in an actual bookstore:

BOOKSTORE CLERK: Can I help you? Are you looking for a particular book?
ME: Yes, I am.
BOOKSTORE CLERK: Do you know the name of the book?
ME: Actually, it doesn't have a name.
BOOKSTORE CLERK: *Please,* leave my store.

Interesting. Next, I tried the same experiment but this time I asked for a book by its title:

BOOKSTORE CLERK: Can I help you? Are you looking for a particular book?
ME: Yes, I am.
BOOKSTORE CLERK: Do you know the name of the book?
ME: Yes. Do you have *The Complete Illustrated History of Cinnamon-Flavored Dental Floss,* the waxed edition?
BOOKSTORE CLERK: *Please, please,* leave my store.

Very interesting.
So what did I learn from my experiments? Well, nothing really. Yes, they did reinforce my hypothesis that a publication

with a name fares far better than one without. But I wanted to do things a little differently—to truly distinguish my opus from the others on those crowded bookstore shelves.

What if my book had a title like the Beatles' *White Album*—just a color instead of a name? Let's say "purple." (I hope you didn't just say "purple" out loud, because if you did you're missing my point.) I imagined this interaction might take place:

BOOK BUYER: Do you have Ellen DeGeneres's new book, it's purple?

BOOKSELLER (a different one than before): It's called *It's Purple?*

BOOK BUYER: No. It's purple. The book is the color purple.

Bookseller: You're looking for Alice Walker's *The Color Purple?*

BOOK BUYER: No, the color of the *book* is purple!

BOOKSELLER: Oh, yes, we *do* have it. Go past the mauve section and you'll find the purple section on your right.

If my book got popular enough, I reasoned, booksellers all over the world would start organizing their books by color. I thought it would be revolutionary, like that Prince fellow who just came out with his highly acclaimed novel *The Book Formerly Known as Volume I.*

Then I had yet another groundbreaking idea. I thought about that saying "You can't judge a book by its cover." Well, what if, I wondered, a book judged *us* instead? I came up with a few judgmental titles that I thought would incite interest in my book:

- My *God*, You're Boring
- You Wouldn't Understand
- It's over Your Head
- Your Mother Swims Out to Meet Troop Ships
- Hey, You There, in the Ugly Shirt

The success of this idea would depend heavily on people valuing the opinion of inanimate objects.

"Wait one minute. Why does that book think I'm wearing an ugly shirt? The nerve of it judging me, just because it's got on that ridiculous book jacket! Hey, Mr. Book, what's with the paper blazer? Goin' to the prom? Where's your cummerbund?" But curiosity and self-doubt would soon set in: "Judge me, will ya, you highfalutin pile of parchment? I'll show you! *I'll buy you and read you!*"

Ka-ching!

I also toyed with the idea of having a one-word title. Like Madonna did. Her book was all about sex so she called it that. I could have called my book *Funny,* or *Funny!,* with an exclamation point, to show people I really mean business. Exclamation points are extremely useful; they give titles energy and vitality. Remember that book a couple years back? *Croutons!* Or the bestselling *PVC Piping!*

Ultimately my journey led me to *The Funny Thing Is*. I liked this title because when you hear it you know you're going to hear an entertaining story. Perfect for essays written by a comic or even a book on the state of Social Security. But it also has another meaning. It's used to explain an ironic situation. Like someone might say, "John just asked me for the money I owed him. Funny thing is, I already paid him back." In this case it's *not* funny because John may have just forgotten the debt had been paid. Or if someone says, "The funny thing is, when I deliberately set fire to the house, the couch was the first thing to go up in flames"; again, that's not funny. That's arson, and it's a felony.

See how versatile it is?

The finishing touch was the three dots after the title (the ellipsis, as we say in bookbiz). My first stab at it was "The Funny Thing Is Dot Dot Dot," but in the end I put real dots instead of words.

The final result: *The Funny Thing Is . . .*

My hope is that this chapter has helped you have a greater appreciation for book titles and a better understanding of all the trouble I went through so you can walk into your neighborhood bookstore, sporting goods outlet, or pawnshop and confidently ask for *The Funny Thing Is . . .* The funny thing is, you probably already did.

that was then or then was that or anyway, it was before now

did you know we have seven hundred TV channels now? It's a wonder we get anything done.

Seven hundred channels—when did this happen? I can remember when I was a kid, we had five channels. And we didn't have a remote. You had to hate something so much that you would be willing to get up and walk five feet to change the channel. If that wasn't enough, you had to guess at the volume, because it was different when you were up close than when you sat back down again. "Damn *Bonanza*—those horses are so much louder when they run!"

It was a different time, it was a simpler time. We were entertained so easily. We would watch anything. We'd watch a flying nun. We'd watch a talking horse. We are so much more sophisticated now, watching people eat bugs and marry strangers for money. Almost makes you miss *Mayberry*, doesn't it? I loved Andy Griffith. By the way, did anything ever happen on that show? When you've got time for whistling, you've got a lot of time.

Commercials used to be six minutes long, and they told us how delicious cigarettes and alcohol were. Man, they were happy smoking and drinking, those people. They're still happy, but they've concentrated all their happiness into thirty seconds now. People in commercials are happy all the time. Especially that woman in the shampoo commercial. She's *too* happy. I don't think our children should see people that happy on television. I fell for it, though—I bought the shampoo. I've got to tell you, I was shampooing for a good half hour . . . and I never got that happy. Finally I just had to fake it.

I get so invested in the lives of those commercial people. Thirty seconds and suddenly you care. That old man who can eat corn on the cob again . . . I'm happy for him. He couldn't eat it for a while. He can now. That woman on jury duty— "Gotta go, gotta go, gotta go right now, gotta go, gotta go, gotta go"—she's gotta *go!* And the judge doesn't understand. I'm so happy by the end of the commercial. "And I don't have to go right now." Ah—fantastic.

So many of the commercials on TV these days are for antidepressants. There are so many—Prozac . . . Paxil . . . And they get you right away. "Are you sad? Do you get stressed? Do you have anxiety?" Yes, yes, and yes. I have all those things. I'm alive.

I don't want to take a pill. If you want to understand real

stress, I say, go to Africa. Go follow some Bushman around. He's getting chased by a lion. *That's* stress! You're not going to find a Pygmy on Paxil, I'll tell you that right now.

But I understand why people need help. The world can be a depressing place. If you want proof, just turn on the news. There you go. Depressing. I was watching the news the other day, "brought to you by Paxil." (That's smart advertising. You watch the news, and suddenly you need it.) When I was a kid the news was on once a day. You either caught it or you missed it. Now the news is on twenty-four hours a day. And that's not enough. There's a guy talking, and there's a crawl going along down there. But that's not all. You've got the guy talking, you've got that crawl going, you're online, you're typing in your opinion on their poll— "No, I say to that, no!" Suddenly you've stopped paying attention to the crawl and you start listening to the guy, and then you look back at the crawl again. You catch the end of something—"Madonna's left foot." What about Madonna's left foot? What happened? You're waiting for it to come back around again, and it goes to commercial. . . . "Are you sad? Do you get stressed . . . ?"

There should just be one crawl that goes around over and over again. "Things are getting worse." That's all we need.

And then there's the local news. They want you to watch every single broadcast they've got. It's not good enough that you're watching the one you're watching. They slip in these teasers that are just so incredibly cruel to get you to watch again later. "It could be the most deadly thing in the world and you may be having it for dinner. We'll tell you what it is, tonight at eleven."

"Is it peas?"

I feel so sorry for newscasters, because they know we can turn off the news. We don't have to watch, but the news is their job. Not only do they have to read the stories, but they don't know what's coming up next. They're just reading the prompter, and they've got to go through a huge range of emotions. They have to jump from one thing to another without flinching. "There were no survivors. . . . And next up: Which candy bar helps you lose weight? Still to come: Is an asteroid headed toward earth? But first, where to find the cheesiest pizza in town! Also, a disturbing new study finds that studies are disturbing."

The newscasters are practically schizophrenic by the end of the broadcast. No wonder they snap by the time they talk to the weatherman. It's like a fantasyland that they enter all of a sudden. "And now let's go to Johnny with the weather. Johnny, when are you gonna stop this rain and bring us some sunshine?"

"I'll stop the rain when you stop the carjackings, Colleen."

The weather is the happiest part of the news. It really is. You know, weathermen are usually very happy people. And at some point they're going to say, "It's a beautiful day" or "It's gonna be a beautiful day." Usually that moment's associated with the weather and sunshine, but it's nice to hear that positive reinforcement even when the crawl underneath the weatherman is telling us unpleasant news. I'd like it if they could incorporate

"It's a beautiful day" into the crawl. Horrible news wouldn't seem as bad if it read, "Get out your sunglasses, 'cause it's a beautiful day for the ozone layer to deplete!" or "It's a beautiful day for the world to explode." That sounds much better.

It seems to me that the crawl actually takes the focus off the entire news team. Back in the days of the "five channels," the anchormen and the weatherman had the spotlight—they were the stars. It was their show and the crawl was something babies and swimmers did . . . on a beautiful day.

ellen's personal home tour

i'd like to take a moment to talk about you, reader. I think it's safe to assume that you have an active imagination. (You're reading a book, that's why I assumed that. And that's also why I'm calling you "reader" and not "Carol" or whatever your given name is.) The imagination is very important in reading. Books are not like television, as I'm sure you've noticed. You have to do a lot of imagining when you read. I bet that's why more people watch TV than read books these days. It's so much easier to have a machine do your imagining for you. But then you have to wonder, *is the easier way always the better way for me?* (I know the answer, but I'm going to let you figure out for yourself. It will be more rewarding for you that way.)

In this chapter I'm going to take advantage of that imagination of yours and take you on a literary tour of my private home, and in the process, I won't have to get my carpets dirty.

Unfortunately, most celebrities don't devote chapters in their books to describing their homes in detail to their fans. So they end up being listed on a "Map to the Stars' Homes" here in Hollywood. Now, I understand why people want to buy those maps. The idea of getting to see where your favorite movie, television, and/or vaudeville star lives is thrilling. I'll admit to you, reader, I bought a "star map" once myself. Ever since I was a girl, it was my lifelong dream to see Ernest Borgnine's driveway from fifty feet away.

The day I moved to Hollywood, I made my dream happen. I saw that long stretch of asphalt partially obstructed by that huge, iron gate and I thought I'd never recover. I mean, *the* Ernest Borgnine! Even his name sounds famous.

I mention this to point out that there's nothing wrong with curiosity. I'm curious to know what your home looks like, too, reader. You, I have a pretty good idea of what you look like. Jean shirt, khaki pants, curled up on your couch with a parrot on your shoulder and your Pekinese, Muffin, panting furiously in your lap. Man, those dogs breathe a lot, don't they? I mean, I know they have to breathe, but I think they overdo it just to get attention. It works, too. Look at how much you ignore that nameless parrot and pay attention to Muffin. And why are those dogs' tongues purple? Or am I thinking of pugs? That's a silly question. How could you know what I'm thinking? You can't; you can only imagine what I'm thinking. But I know what you're thinking right now: *How could she know exactly what I'm wearing and what I'm doing? Is she some kind of wizard?* I know it's creepy, but it's not wizardry. You don't win an Emmy for comedy writing by *not* knowing your audience.

Anyway, let's not stand here on the threshold any longer. Welcome to my home. Let me just get the door here. . . . I've got the key, right . . . ummm, this key ring is so confusing. . . . Okay, wait . . . here it is. . . . No, that's the key to the maid's quarters . . . the chauffeur's quarters . . . my personal training facility . . . bowling alley . . . Here we go! The front door! Once again, welcome to my home! One second . . . this lock is a little sticky . . . stupid lock. . . . There. And here we are! Finally! The front foyer!

Now, I wanted to make this a very warm, welcoming room, so I covered it from floor to ceiling in tan shag carpet. Isn't it nice and quiet? And it gets very warm in the summer. I've had people tell me that once they walk into this room, they don't want to go into the rest of the house. Isn't that nice?

I like this room the most because you can't break anything in here. Not even if you try! You could throw a vase straight up into the air and it would just hit the ceiling, bounce off a wall, land on the floor, and not even have the tiniest chip in it. And the whole thing would take place in complete silence.

There's a spiral staircase on our right that leads up to the second floor, but we're not going to be visiting that floor today. I don't mean to sound bossy. It's just that I have to set boundaries. And, if I asked you where you wanted to go, I'd have to go the way you wanted to go, but if another person read this and wanted to go, say, to the rumpus room in the basement, then I'd have to write another version of this book for them. Another version would mean the cover photo would have to be slightly different and I would have to add a ".01" to the title or something to signify that it was a new version of the book. I don't think it would work to put one of those yellow stars that say ALL NEW VERSION on the cover because really, the rest of the book would be the same, except for this one chapter.

I mean, I can't open up the possibility that every chapter could be customized for every reader. It would make me seem insecure. When you have an idea, you've gotta stick to it!

My grandma used to shout that at me when I was a child. I knew she was trying to be supportive, but why did she have to shout it? She never yelled at my brother. She'd just creep into his room at night and whisper, "All that glitters is not gold." Come to think of it, maybe I got off lucky, because he's been scared of anything glittery ever since. It's really very sad. He lives a glitter-free half life. He can't ever go to Mardi Gras. Children don't want to do arts and crafts with him. He can't even look at a piñata. But hey! This isn't a chapter about my brother's grandma-induced neuroses, it's about my beautiful home.

So, let me throw open these French doors and lead you into my living room. To the left, the length of the wall is covered with that nature-scenery wallpaper like they used to have at the dentist's office when I was a kid. This particular scene is a lake in autumn; beautiful fiery reds and oranges, with the calm of the dark blue lake in the background. It's gorgeous and scuff-resistant.

That sets the perfect tone for my sunken conversation pit, the centerpiece of the room. These were very popular back in the seventies, when people were really interested in talking. I find now they're just as useful for drinking and waiting for dinner to be served. All the furniture in the pit is brown and the carpeting is a dark apricot. I wanted the overall effect to be pit-like, but most people don't get it. A lot of people assume I'm colorblind.

To the right, I have a wall of floor-to-ceiling windows that look out over my professional Ping-Pong court. Comedy is my life, but Ping-Pong is my passion. It's great to sit in here in the summer and watch a match. If you're in the pit, you're watching at about knee level but that's when you realize the game of Ping-Pong is all in the knees. It's awe inspiring.

Let's plow ahead and go into this back hallway. The kitchen is on our left, but there's nothing too exciting in there to show you, unless you love sponges. I had everything in my kitchen made of sponge. That way, the spill cleans itself up and no one ever cuts their finger. But it's not that interesting, just very bouncy to walk around in.

Now, this back hallway stretches one hundred yards in both directions. This not only helps reduce sound when I'm having late-night parties and babysitting, but I can also do my wind sprints without having to go outside. These are the things you dream of when you're house hunting, but you don't think you'll ever actually find.

At the end of each hallway are matching guest bedrooms that have been decorated to be the mirror images of each other. I loved this idea when I thought of it, until I realized I had to look at one room, walk two hundred yards, look at the other room, and then think about how they were the same—but opposite. It's not as "freaky" as I wanted it to be. It kind of just seems like a hotel.

This first guest bathroom here to our right has its own shower, sauna, and karaoke machine. I know it sounds extravagant, but it was here when I moved in. I think it's the perfect combination: You can take a sauna to warm up your vocal cords and free your throat of any phlegm, then hop into the shower and crank up the karaoke machine for some of the best shower singing you've ever done in your life. It's the kind of setup I never knew I needed before, and now I can't live without it.

In fact, a lot of the really fancy stuff here, like the second-floor Olympic-size swimming pool and the tanning bed breakfast nook, came with the house. The man who had this house built was the guy who invented "doing lunch." Apparently, he made a mint off of that idea, so when he was designing his new dream home, the sky was the limit. He lived here for two years and then got an idea for a dreamier dream home. That happens all the time here in Hollywood. Dreams are a dime a dozen and so are the homes that are built because of them.

So that's the whole tour! I mean, I could show you the grounds but I don't want to get my slippers all grimy. Besides, the gardeners haven't trimmed the topiaries in a while, so the hedge that's supposed to look like a dolphin looks like a dolphin with a beard and pants.

Here, I'll just have you picture a beautiful garden, whatever a "beautiful garden" means to you—and then spray some Glade. That's just what my backyard is like! In fact, that's what everyone's backyard is like in Hollywood.

Thank you for coming into my humble home, reader. I hope it was all you imagined it would be, *and more!* Now, if I could just ask you to let yourself out that screen door right past the stained-glass window depicting me performing live onstage, it would be such a help.

Toodle-loo!

things to be grateful for

I'd read somewhere that it's good to keep a gratitude journal. We forget how many great things there are in our lives and when you start jotting them down and really get introspective about even the littlest of things, it's amazing how all the terrible things in life don't seem as bad.

Gratitude can surprise you. Once you start seeing things in a positive way, you can make almost anything seem like a gift.

At first it's difficult to get to the things that matter. My journal started off like this:

I'm grateful for air—I need it to breathe.
I'm grateful for food—I need it to live.
I'm grateful for water—it's what my body is 80% of.

Then, after listing five pages of life-sustaining needs, I became angry with my journal (as you probably already are) and decided I needed to dig a little deeper.

Animals don't talk. At first I thought, *Oh, that's a shame, poor things can't communicate to us.* But then I thought, *If some* people *are annoying, think about how bad it would be to come home from work and listen to your dog or cat tell you what it did all day long.*

First, your pet would berate you for not paying enough attention to it.

"Well, it's about time! It seems like you've been gone forever. I have no concept of time and I'm aging faster than you, you'd think you'd want to spend as much time with me as you could. Why'd you even get me? To pet once in a while? Oh! Thank you, master. Look, I'm bored. I have this one flea that is driving me nuts. I give and give and give. I'm your best friend, I love you unconditionally, and what do you do for me? Oh, you feed me. That same boring dry food every day. I see what you eat. You think I'm stupid? I know there's variety in your meals, but I, for some reason, don't deserve anything but this monotony."

Then the animal would go into a longwinded, boring monologue about the day.

"Okay, this morning there is this bird outside chirping and chirping and chirping and so I start barking, right? And the bitch woman next door screams, "Shut up" to me. She doesn't tell the stupid bird to shut up, just me. So I barked a few more times just to piss her off. I mean, she can't tell me what to do, you know what I'm saying? I hate her. Then, I heard something a few blocks away, so I started barking again—and guess what? Yep, she started yelling at me again. It's not like she doesn't make noise of her own. She's got the TV on all day long, all the talk shows . . . and she thinks I'm loud? Those people on TV yell at each other constantly and when they do the audience applauds and cheers? Give me a break. I'm supposed to just lie around and make no noise? Oh, I don't know. Maybe I'm just in a bad mood. I think I'll just have a biscuit and head to bed. . . . Hop to it! I can't get it myself!"

It turns out the main reason I love dogs is that they don't talk.

Before my gratitude journal began, there were things out in the world that I wished never existed, like mosquitoes. Mosquitoes, especially at night, are the most annoying thing I can think of. I know there is some scientific explanation for why even the mosquito plays a part in balancing out nature, but that doesn't make up for the fact that many times I've spent the better part of what was supposed to be a good night's sleep hunting those bloodsuckers down. Then I thought, "Wait a minute . . . that's what being grateful is all about. It's about the mosquito and the fly and other bothersome creatures. If we didn't have them, what would I complain about?" Who wants a world where there isn't a reason to complain?

There are people in this world who never complain. "Hey, you know Bob's girlfriend, Cheryl? She never complains about anything. Isn't that great?" What am I supposed to talk to her about? Eventually, that's how people bond. What a boring relationship if every conversation went, "You like humidity? Me, too."

"I love when mosquitoes bite me, it reminds me I'm alive!"

"You know what doesn't bother me? Frostbite . . . Yeah, it makes me forget I have fingers for a while."

Small talk would be impossible.

"Boy, it sure is a hot one today."

"It's how reptiles thrive."

"Yes, but my skin doesn't shed."

"Yes, it does, we couldn't live if it didn't."

"Good-bye."

Small talk is something I used to dread. Now, since I've found ways to be grateful, I realize that without small talk people at parties would just stare at each other and eat twice as many chips. I go to a lot of parties—I would be huge! Now I love to start up a conversation with someone and discover, through small talk, where they live. How fascinating.

"How long have you lived in Pigeon Acres?"

"Oh, for about six years."

"Is it nice?"

"We love it."

"Great. I'm gonna go talk to that guy over there about how unseasonably cold it is this summer."

"Okay, I should probably stand by the crudités platter and discuss where to buy the freshest vegetables."

"Isn't it fantastic we aren't just staring at each other?"

"Yeah, this is a really good party."

My gratitude journal is turning out to be an exercise in tolerance.

I locked myself out of the house the other day and I used the time as a chance to get to know my neighbors.

I stubbed my toe on my table and realized I should wear shoes inside.

My cat knocked over my plant and it made me hang all my plants. Now I have more room for books and candles!

Gratitude is about taking that frown and turning it upside down. How can you turn a frown upside down when it is already down? It should be upside up. Gratitude is looking on the brighter side of life, even if it means hurting your eyes. Gratitude is something we can learn from others if they will talk to you.

Gratitude is appreciating the things we can't have, like a talking dog.

my self-conscious

or

Check Me Out!

One of the best pieces of advice I have ever been given is, "Don't care too much about what other people think, or you'll never do anything." Well, that's fine to say, but it's really hard to do without feeling self-conscious. Some people really, truly don't care what other people think, and I say, "Good for them!" There are guys walking around in bicycle shorts and that's it! It's quite a bit to look at and difficult *not* to look at, all at the same time. Yet they couldn't care less.

I've decided the key to doing whatever you want—and I've been interviewed on this subject hundreds of times—is standing out but fitting in. That's what it is. Take fashion, for instance. You don't want to wear something so wild that, God forbid, somebody notices. But you also don't want to choose the kind of outfit that someone else could be wearing—like when you both show up at a party in exactly the same thing. That's embarrassing! I don't know if it has happened to you, but it has happened to me—twice. Both times it was William Shatner. And you want to know something? I think I look better in a tube top and I'll say it.

The way I dress is kind of boring. I don't care. I don't go for all the trendy stuff. I don't understand it, really. Sometimes I think that fashion designers are just trying to see what they can get away with. They want to see if you're willing to dress up like a circus clown or a prostitute or, worse yet, a circus prostitute. You know, they come up with some of these things like the sarong or the sari. It is the same thing, I think, and if not, I'm sarong. Sari.

There was a time when shopping involved an actual dressing *room.* There were four walls, and you entered through a door. A whole door! And you could close the door and you could try on clothes and cry or whatever you do in the dressing room. But you had a door. There is no door any longer.

You go to try on clothes and the door is just getting higher and higher up and lower and lower down. Essentially, you are trying to get dressed behind a two-by-four. You know everyone can see the underwear going down around your ankles. (I don't know about you, but I always take my underwear off no matter what I'm trying on. Just a habit, really.)

They've made the door tiny so the salesperson can get to you. They couldn't before. They would just be lurking outside the door. "Can I get you anything? Need anything? Everything all right? How is everything? Can I get you anything? My name's Rachel if you need me. I'm a Capricorn, so I love to help people. My uncle's in prison for a crime he didn't commit. I love Ally McBeal. Did you see it last week? I have an eating disorder and won't admit it. Do you think I'm pretty? I hate my job. Can I run away with you? Do you know Tom Cruise? Would he think I'm pretty?"

Now she can just poke her head right in there. "Can I get you anything? How is everything? Need anything? Everything all right?"

"I said I would call you, Rachel. I don't need anything."

All that checking in. What could go so wrong that they need to check on you that often? "My bra is in my ass . . . ! *Rachel!*"

I'd like to see how far they would go to help you if you did tell them your bra was in your ass. "Oh, my. It is in the ass? So do you need a different size or color?"

And they've also taken the mirror out of the dressing room, so that you are forced to walk out to take a look at yourself. This is so they can get another shot at you. They are there to tell you how nice you look since you don't have opinions of your own.

"That looks fabulous."

"Really?"

"Yes. Your ass looks fabulous."

That's how they get you. If they tell you your ass looks good, you are buying it. "That blouse makes your ass look fabulous. Is that your bra? Well, it makes your ass look *fabulous!*"

The ass is such an important thing now. We check out our

ass like crazy when we try on clothes. Not only do we check out our ass, but our entire facial expression changes when we do. We make the ass face. *That is my ass.* You turn a different way. *That is my ass that way.* Then you start to walk away. *I'm going to walk away and that is my ass.*

We don't make the ass face when we are at home naked looking at ourselves in the mirror. Totally different face then.

I'm amazed by people who are just so comfortable with their nakedness. It doesn't matter what they look like. They are just totally comfortable being naked. I admire that in people.

I think the people who are the most comfortable being naked are those people who videotape themselves having sex. You've got to be so confident about your body to be videotaping your sex. Because no matter how much your partner loves you, in the heat of everything, stuff is moving so fast and at so many different angles, it's not going to be pretty. When you watch the videotape later, you risk your partner saying, "I never saw that before. Have you seen that thing you do, yourself, right there? That thing . . . right there."

People who videotape their sex are doing it for only one of two reasons. Maybe they're doing it because they are so egotistical that they love nothing more than watching themselves. "Look at us. We are *hot!* Look at us. . . . Look at us! Ooh . . . look at me. Look at me! Look at *you.* Look at me again. Look . . . look . . . look. Look at me!"

Or maybe people tape themselves so they can watch the playback together like football players, looking for ways to improve their performance the next time. "All right. Let's take a look right here, shall we? Okay. Here is what I'm talking about. See how your elbow is up so high and your back is arched right there? Not the best time to do that. I think I'd hold out on that until . . . there. That is when you should do it—right . . . *there.* Okay. And what is going on right here? What is happening, I'll tell you. Nothing. A lot of energy. A lot of energy. A lot of energy. Look at my face. Nothing. Nothing going on. Nothing! You might want to kick in once in a while. You know what I'm saying. Now, I know I'm biting my lip. That's to keep from laughing. Where did you come up with *that* little technique? Did you make that up? I thought so. Don't do it. Okay? Don't cry. . . . Come on! This is how we learn! Let's get back in there and try it again. Come on. What do you mean, you're not in the mood?"

I don't know. I don't understand a lot of the stuff people are into but I do believe that everyone has the right to do whatever they want with their bodies. If it makes you feel good, do it. It's your life and it's your body. As long as there are two consenting adults—or three or five sometimes, I guess.

I just don't understand a lot of it.

Like people who are into the Mile High Club. You know, those people who have sex in a bathroom on a plane. I don't understand that. First of all, I have questions. How do you even fit two people in there to have sex? I mean, I barely have room to have sex in there by myself. I have to leave the door open a smidgen because my leg has to be . . . you know . . . just so. That's how I like it.

Sex should bring people together but sometimes it really separates them. We have this huge debate going on right now about same-sex marriage. There are people who are against it. There are people who are for it. And the people who are against it say marriage is a union between a man and a woman and it has always been that way and it should always remain that way. If we change the law to include two people of the same sex, they say, then what will be next? Someone could marry an *animal.* That is where they go right away. These people scare me. They think *we're* weird.

I don't want to marry a goat. I really don't. I can't imagine even dating a goat—getting to the point that you're serious enough to make that kind of a commitment. Sure, you can live together for a little while to figure it out, see if you are compatible . . .

I'm just picturing the apartment you'd have, you and the goat. Photographs all over the place—you and the goat on the beach running, holding hands. You and the goat being serenaded by mariachis at a restaurant. You and the goat in front of the Eiffel Tower eating crepes and tin cans. You and the goat making faces in a strip from the photo booth.

Sunday morning you'll be trying to read the paper; the goat is trying to eat it. "Don't you eat that section. I haven't read that yet! Don't you eat. . . . Don't you eat . . . Come here! I love you, you goat."

I think it would be a tough day even for the most open-minded parents if you brought the goat home. "Mom, Dad, this is Billy. We are in love."

I guess what I'm trying to say is, there are a lot of self-righteous people out there. And if you try to adjust your life to please them—by the way you dress, your sexuality, or the ass faces you like to make—you're just going to go crazy and risk being as unhappy as these self-righteous kooks are.

So enjoy your life. God gave us our bodies as a gift. (Granted, to some of us it's kind of a gag gift, but that's okay too.) Wear what you want, love who you want, and have fun.

the last chapter

There are so many different ways to end a book.

There are some people out there who love the ending the best. In fact, they'll buy a book and go straight for the ending. (If everyone were like that, I could have saved myself some time and *just* written the ending. Maybe that'll be my next book.)

The people who just like to read the last page might like a traditional ending. So, since I like to try to please everyone (I know they say "you can't please all of the people all of the time," but, by God, I'll die trying), here goes. . . .

When Mama saw what I had done, she gathered up all her muster and with a huge smile on her face said, "Ellen, if you've said that once, you've said it a million times!" As we looked at each other with those faces that only a mother and daughter could recognize, we pulled off our aprons, threw them on the counter, and I said, "Mama, let's me and you get a cherry soda." It was that day I knew my life had just begun.

No. That is the worst ending I've ever read. I don't even know what "muster" means. How about this:

As I pulled out of my driveway and into the hazy California sun, I realized that had I not found my true essence, I would never have had the courage to leave all that I had known behind. It was that day I knew my life had just begun.

Mmm. Still not doing it for me. Maybe I should incorporate both endings, like so:

As I pulled out of my driveway and into the lazy (I like that better than "hazy") California sun, my mother waved good-bye to me with a cherry soda in her hand and a smile on her face that only a daughter could recognize. She pulled off her apron and threw it at my car. And it was that day I knew my life had just begun . . . with muster.

Good night.

bonus chapter

5 % more words,
absolutely free!*

They say that there's no free lunch; that everything comes with a price tag. (If you don't believe me, try shoplifting something.) But not this chapter. This chapter is 100% completely free! In actuality, my book ends on page 172. But not for you.

You (and only you) get pages 173–177 as my way of saying "thank you" for buying my book. (If you didn't buy this book and are reading a friend's copy, don't be greedy. Maybe you should save this Extra Special Bonus Chapter for the person who actually plunked down the cash.)

These days it does seem like we're all hooked on getting more, forever scouting around for that little something extra: more long-distance minutes, increased legroom, more free

* After mail-in rebate.

Tibet, and bigger supersize sodas. I personally get a thrill out of getting something for nothing, whether it's shampoo that comes bundled with a free conditioner or when my dentist offers a two-for-one tooth-pulling special. I just love a great deal.

Speaking of sweet deals, there's nothing as sweet as free sugar. Restaurants put it right there on the table. All you can eat! That goes for all condiments. If restaurants did charge for them it would make figuring out the bill awfully hard. "Let see, I had the burger, you had the dollop of ketchup; I had the squeeze of mustard, a cup of coffee, a pinch of pepper, and one-point-five packets of sugar. Wait a minute. Excuse me. Waitress? There seems to be a mistake on our bill. We didn't use any salt."

The savvy shopper can even find complimentary gifts when looking for a new home. Once, my Realtor showed me a house and gleefully announced it had a "bonus room." Where's the bonus in that? It's already part of the house. Isn't it? Is the roof a bonus too?

"Boy, we really lucked out on our house; it came with bonus indoor plumbing."

So what is the bonus of this bonus chapter, you might be asking yourself? (If you're not asking yourself that, maybe you should. I'll wait.) Well, I had to ask myself the same question. What extra special something could I give my readers? Practical information on making life easier? Maybe some tips on getting stains out of carpet or how to change a tire? To be honest, I'd be the last person who should be doling out gardening advice. I don't have the patience for growing things. Yes, I realize there's nothing quite as satisfying as eating food that you've pulled up from the ground and that's why, at the height of the planting season, I bury cans of tomato soup in my backyard and dig them up again in late spring.

No, to be a real bonus, it's got to be something that you couldn't get anywhere else. Like the answers to the most baffling unanswered questions of the universe. And it just so happens I have those answers. (One of the many perks of being a celebrity is that "the answers" are sent directly to your agent; the better your career is going the more answers you get—that's how they get you.)

So what are we waiting for?

Presenting

The Extra Special Bonus Chapter

The Top 5 Mysteries of the World Explained

*(Brought to you in an extra special font
that's completely different from the rest of the book!)*

1) Do Aliens really exist?

Yes, they are cleverly disguised as birds. Remember that old adage: Every time a bell rings an alien gets its wings?

2) How were the pyramids built?

They were built over a span of ten thousand years, because that's how long it takes to find a reliable contractor.

3) How big is the universe?

It's as big as an angel dancing on the head of a pin, provided that pin is two thousand trillion miles wide.

4) Are crop circles a hoax?

No. The actual crops are the hoax. They are created by bored, yet highly motivated, teenagers in rural areas who "plant" the artificial "crops" under the darkness of night.

5) Where did I leave my keys?

I'm sorry, you're on your own with this one. I don't have time to help you tear apart the house looking for them. Why, oh why, can't you just put them in the same place every time?

But wait . . . there's more!

The Extra Special Bonus Chapter: Special Bonus Lottery Numbers Guaranteed to Win

That's right, these numbers, in combination with other numbers, can help you win the lottery. Next time you play the lottery, use one of the numbers below with other numbers you pick and you might have a winner!

1) 1	6) 6
2) 2	7) 7
3) 3	8) 8
4) 4	9) 9
5) 5	10) 0

Good luck!

I hope you have enjoyed this bonus chapter, because now it's over. There is really nothing else to read in this book, except the Library of Congress information, but that's in every book. It's hard to say good-bye, but it's time. Good-bye. Or "Adieu" or "Ciao." Those are just some of the languages I know how to say good-bye in. I don't have time for the others, as my book is now over.

But first, let's review the bonus chapter. It's a free chapter; people love deals; houses have a bonus room; and the universe is expanding (that wasn't in the book, but it's true and actually that is just one more bonus for you).

The ending of a book is like saying good-bye to a good friend or relative—that is, if you read the end. And this is the end. If you can't stand the thought of it ending, maybe you could have somebody hide the book right now, before the end.

Or don't read this last line, which would mean you didn't read the end of this book.

about the author

ELLEN DEGENERES's first book, *My Point . . . And I Do Have One,* was an instant national bestseller that spent more than six months on the *New York Times* bestseller list. DeGeneres has won an Emmy Award, a Peabody Award, and a People's Choice Award for her work as a writer and actress on her television series *Ellen* and received Emmy nominations as host of the *39th Annual Grammy Awards* and as an executive producer of her critically accclaimed one-woman HBO special *The Beginning.* DeGeneres made history when her on-screen persona Ellen Morgan became the first openly gay leading character on television, but her groundbreaking legacy had already begun in 1986, on *The Tonight Show,* when she became the first and only female comic invited by Johnny Carson to sit down with him after her stand-up performance. In September 2003, DeGeneres launched her own daytime talk show. In its first season, *The Ellen DeGeneres Show* won four Daytime Emmys, including the award for Best Talk Show.